"On Purpose For A Purpose"

*A Study based on the lives of Esther,
Queen of Persia, and Mordecai, the Jew whose
stories are found in the Old Testament.*

by
Shelley Hendrix

www.xulonpress.com

Dedicated to My Husband, Stephen Hendrix—
Your love has inspired me to dream big and
has allowed me to experience more fully the love of Christ.
I still can't believe I get to be married to Stephen Hendrix!

"If we love one another God dwells in us and His love is
perfected in us." I John 4:12

And to my children,
Amelia, Macey, Jackson, & the ones I get to meet in
Heaven—
I am so thankful God gave us to one another, On Purpose
for a Purpose!

"I have no greater joy than to hear that my children walk
in truth." III John 4

- *"Shelley Hendrix has succeeded in offering this biblically sound study that offers great spiritual insight. The lessons are sometimes hard-hitting, yet wrapped in a warm, personal story or a gentle warning that conveys respect and love to the reader. Shelley has done a great job balancing so many aspects of writing to produce a helpful study that will be enjoyed by many."*

  Dr. Lori Salierno, Nationally recognized speaker and author, and Founder and CEO of Celebrate Life International, Inc. (www.celebratelife.org)

- *"In a day when teaching seems to lack both dynamic and content, Shelley Hendrix offers a wonderful combination of both."*

  Ken Davis, Nationally recognized comedian, author, speaker, and President of the Dynamic Communicator's Workshop (www.kendavis.com)

- *"Biblical, passionate, anointed, practical teaching that gets right down to where we are—challenging and awakening with such convicting, life impacting power that is obviously the Lord, describes the incredibly gifted and Spirit-filled personality that is Shelley Hendrix...Shelley is God's love gift and messenger to the churches of our day, calling us back to the ultimate reality: a close and intimate walk with Jesus Christ..."*

Heather Steele, Pastor's wife and leader in the First Ladies Ministry of Holmes Creek Baptist Church, Chipley, FL

Acknowledgments

There are so many wonderful people I want to thank. First, and above all, thank you to my gracious Heavenly Father for every experience, every relationship, every single breath You sovereignly ordained and used to bring me to Yourself. Thank you for showing me so compassionately that You have put me here on purpose for a purpose.

Thank you to my husband, my children, and my family who continually encourage me to step out of my areas of comfort and follow God's guidance in my life to go deeper with Jesus.

Thank you to my Pastor, Dr. Johnny Hunt, for instilling in me a passion for God's Word. You have enriched my life more than I could ever adequately convey.

Thank you to Dr. Lori Salierno, for your willingness to read this manuscript, give feedback, offer suggestions and encouragement. Your life motivates me to live a life of intention and purpose.

Thank you to Mrs. Katharine Brown, for your wonderful job editing this manuscript. Your willingness to use your giftedness to bring about a finished book has been an incredible blessing.

Thank you to Jack Walton at Xulon Press for all of your advice and all of your encouragement to keep writing and working on this book.

And, last but not least, to the wonderful people who are involved in Mary's Vineyard Ministries, Inc. Your support, prayers, encouragement, and advice have already made an eternal impact and will continue to do so. May you be richly rewarded by the Lord!

Foreword

$\mathcal{P}$eriodically, a writer will come along that you have
had the opportunity to know as much about their character as you do their writing. This happens to be the case
with Shelley Hendrix. I have had the privilege of knowing
Shelley and her husband for many years, and to have known
both of them before they met and married each other. Shelley
writes from a life of experience. She has chosen the person of
Esther, along with other characters from this wonderful book,
to write *"On Purpose For A Purpose."* This is a Bible study
that will encourage every person who reads it. It will be of
a great help especially to the ladies who are teaching God's
Word or who desire to go to another level. I think that you
will find it not only biblically accurate, but you will also find
some fresh thoughts that have been derived from Shelley's
heart which has been molded in the crucible that God has
allowed her to live in through the years past. Take experience,
integrity, character, and place her skills of writing alongside
of it, and you will hold in your hands one great book!

It is my prayer that each of you will not only read this, but
consider using it for a Bible study with a group of ladies, or
in the small group program of your Church. I believe that you

will be encouraged, challenged, and stretched. There will be times that you will laugh, and other times you will weep. You will think of others when you read this book, but at the same time I believe your heart will be filled with emotion as it strikes very close to home.

May God bless you as you read, and then pass along, the truth of this book.

Blessings!

Dr. Johnny Hunt, Pastor
First Baptist Church Woodstock
Woodstock, GA

Preface

$\mathscr{A}$s I studied the story of Esther in my time alone with the Lord in the fall of 2005, I had no idea how much her story would come to mean to me. Esther has always been one of my favorite biblical characters, and the story of how God used her to save her people has always been very special to me. There have been many times that those famous words of Mordecai have been used by God in my life to help me walk in obedience when a decision to make was a difficult one: "*For such a time as this…*"

As I read through this wonderful book in the Old Testament of the Bible in 2005, I thought what God was showing me was just for me. I thought the lessons that were so personal would speak loudest and clearest to my heart alone. Little did I know He would lead me to share those truths with other women; first in my Sunday School class, then with women at conferences, and then as a 12-week Bible Study. I have been overwhelmed by the response of those who have chosen to walk through this study with me. We have so much more in common that most of us realize.

Let's be honest, there are already so many wonderfully written Bible studies on Esther. I have wondered many times why God would have me write yet another one. I can only offer this answer. I have written this because He told me to. He has faithfully led me one step at a time in every area of my life and ministry, and so this is, quite simply and honestly, the next step. This study has become such a big part of my life and has ministered to me personally in countless ways. I pray that God will use the lessons contained in this book to challenge and encourage you in your own journey with our Lord and Savior, Jesus Christ.

For those of you who may be reading this as a person who is still not sure about the whole "Jesus thing", I want you to know I am honored by your investment of time and thought in reading. My hope is that you will read this with your eyes wide open to what God may be trying to show you about Himself. God makes a promise in the Bible that if we will seek Him, we will find Him, if we'll seek Him with our whole heart.

Something I want to ask you to keep in mind while reading this book is that so many times, when we read about people in Scripture, we fail to give adequate attention to the truth that these were indeed ***REAL LIFE*** people. Some of us have become so accustomed to the stories, that we become somewhat numb to the humanity of the characters. These are not merely characters in a story. They are real people whose real stories have been passed down all these generations because God has something to tell us through their lives. As you read through this book and through her story, remind yourself regularly that Esther is a *real* person. When she was taken from her home to be a part of the king's harem of women, she felt the emotions of that reality. When she was chosen to be queen, she felt the gamut of feelings that would understandably come from such an event. Both Mordecai and Esther lived their lives, one minute at a time, with twenty-four hours in their days, and had to live out their story over years—the story we can read in one sitting! Keep this reality in mind as you move from chapter to chapter.

In this Bible Study, my desire is that we would discover the freedom of finding our identity in Christ versus finding our identity in the external realities in our lives. I want us to be closer to God as a result of hearing from Him during our time with Him. I pray this will be a life-changing investment of your time in your relationship with the Lord. There may be parts of this study that are painful for you to walk through. That is not my intention. The last thing I would ever want to do is hurt anyone by what I teach or write. I do, however, realize that God will use what causes us pain to strengthen our faith in Him if we'll just let Him. I pray you will be willing to take an honest look at yourself as you look into the mirror of God's Word. God's Word is called the Sword of the Spirit, and it is a double-edged sword. One side wounds with the truth, the other heals with grace.

The truth can be very painful. God allows pain in our lives to change us and to make us mature as the people God has created us to be. His process may be painful, but He is never just out to hurt us. There is always a greater purpose for our pain than what we can see while we're going through it, and He truly is working all these things together for *our good*. Everything about our lives is ***on purpose for a purpose***. The pleasant experiences, as well as the painful ones, are part of God's good plan.

I am so thankful you have picked up this book, and I pray with all sincerity that God will minister mightily to you through it.

Because He First Loved Me,

Shelley

Table of Contents

"*They that can give up essential liberty to obtain a little temporary safety deserve neither liberty nor safety*". *Benjamin Franklin.*

CHAPTER 1

It's My Party and I'll Divorce My Wife If I Want To! **(Part 1)**

❧

*O*ur story begins like a lot of fairy tales begin. There's a strong and powerful king. There's an unknown and beautiful maiden who finds herself chosen from among the many; a maiden with incredible odds to defy and overcome. There is an older, wiser mentor for the main character. And, as in any great story, there is also a wicked enemy and overwhelming obstacles to face. The big difference, however, between fairy tales and this story, is that this one is actually, *and completely*, true! The best stories, in my opinion, are always the ones that happened in real life. These are the stories that speak most to my heart and mind. As much as I love a good fictional story, (especially the ones children make up), there is simply nothing like reading or hearing of someone's real life experiences. To read how a real person overcame real obstacles gives me hope that the same can happen for me.

This true story found in the pages of Old Testament Scripture is loved by so many people, and I believe it is so because so many of us can identify with it on different levels, regardless of our age, background, financial portfolio, national heritage, etc.

Our story, like most fairy tales, begins in a castle...

Esther 1: 1-8

"¹IT WAS in the days of Ahasuerus [Xerxes], the Ahasuerus who reigned from India to Ethiopia over 127 provinces. ²In those days when King Ahasuerus sat on his royal throne which was in Shushan or Susa [the capital of the Persian Empire] in the palace or castle, ³In the third year of his reign he made a feast for all his princes and his courtiers. The chief officers of the Persian and Median army and the nobles and governors of the provinces were there before him ⁴While he showed the riches of his glorious kingdom and the splendor and excellence of his majesty for many days, even 180 days. ⁵And when these days were completed, the king made a feast for all the people present in Shushan the capital, both great and small, a seven-day feast in the court of the garden of the king's palace. ⁶There were hangings of fine white cloth, of green and of blue [cotton], fastened with cords of fine linen and purple to silver rings or rods and marble pillars. The couches of gold and silver rested on a [mosaic] pavement of porphyry, white marble, mother-of-pearl, and [precious] colored stones. ⁷Drinks were served in different kinds of golden goblets, and there was royal wine in abundance, according to the liberality of the king." (Amplified Bible Translation)

King Ahasuerus, also known as Xerxes, after a few years of reigning over such a vast empire, decides to throw a party. It was not just your run-of-the-mill royal party—as elaborate as that would have been on its own—Noooo! He throws an extravagant, lengthy party—one that lasted about 6 months. There were parties within a party, as guests were coming and going. Several possibilities are given for his reason for throwing such an elaborate party, but suffice it to say, he did it because he could. There was no real purpose given in these verses. It is believed that perhaps he was throwing this party in hopes to gain favor and support for his military plans to go to war with Greece. He wanted to prove he had the finances to go to war with such a powerful nation as Greece was in those days. Other than this, I'm not sure there was much more reason than for the king to feel good about himself—his power, his wealth, his possessions. Perhaps he was bored with life—it's hard to imagine, but even wealthy, powerful people can get bored. We know that he wanted to show off everything he had. If he was planning to go to war, it begs the question (to me anyway) "Why?" Maybe he felt this would bring the excitement he longed to feel again. This was a king driven by power. There are other historical accounts of his bizarre behavior and it all points to the reality that this was a king who did not know God. We are created to be worshipers, not to be worshipped. If we're not worshiping God, we will find someone or something else to worship, and oftentimes, *we pick ourselves* as our object of worship. This seems to be the case with King Ahasuerus.

I read a story of another familiar king recently. Even though he died before I knew who he was, his life is known worldwide and his fame is unmatched. His name was Elvis Presley. In an article I picked up while waiting for my bi-annual teeth cleaning at my dentist's office, I read these words spoken by his wife Priscilla Presley in an excerpt from a book she co-authored called <u>Elvis by the Presley's:</u>

"Most entertainers with his talent simply accept the talent. Elvis wanted to know why it was given to him; why he was the object of such adoration; why blessing fell on him; and—perhaps most crucially, why he still couldn't define his ultimate purpose. He was convinced his purpose went well beyond music and movies."(Ladies' Home Journal, August 2005) Elvis wanted to know the purpose behind his life. I believe he would have found it had he not given in to all the pressure and gone back to his roots and his faith in God. Reread the description of the fancy and priceless décor of King Ahasuerus: He had the finest the world had to offer in his day—finer than what I have in my house today for sure! Not understanding that "to whom much is given, much is required", not realizing that his position held enormous potential for helping others by being a servant leader, he settled for wanting the approval and applause of the ones around him. Simply living a life of luxury and royalty was not enough. Perhaps he was bored.

In Dr. Larry Crabb's book, <u>The Marriage Builder,</u> he writes about each person's God-given needs for security and significance. He states, and I agree, that we are all born with these two built-in hunger pangs. Just like the other drives God places within us, such as hunger so that we will eat, and thirst so that we will quench it with water that our body needs for survival, He placed these two needs within us. Just like our hunger drives us to food and our thirst to water, these drives for security and significance will force us to find the source that will give us security (that somehow, in some way all will be well) and a sense of significance (a *purpose* for existing; a reason to *really* live, not just exist). So, just as God gives us hunger so we will eat, and thirst so that we will drink in order to survive—He gives us these two main spiritual needs in order to draw us to Him. HE alone will satisfy those cravings. There IS NO REAL LIFE apart from Christ.

I've read about people with some really strange cravings. Just think about the wild cravings we can experience during pregnancy. If you have never experienced this, you probably know at least one person who has. One of the things I craved intensely with my son was marinara sauce—I would have poured it over cereal and ice cream if I had thought I could get away with it! There are cravings of all sorts and for all kinds of reasons. There are some people who crave dirt, for example. This eating disorder is called "Pica". Why dirt? Often times, it is because their bodies are deficient of a certain mineral, like zinc or iron, and they are *temporarily* satisfied when they eat dirt. Of course, dirt doesn't truly satisfy them; it wasn't created for this purpose. Once they are treated for their eating disorder, and are given supplements, when there isn't a case of some other mental illness, the craving and ingestion of dirt ends. They find the source that was created to meet the need, and no longer need to settle for dirt.

How many of us are living with temporal satisfaction and a drive for more because we aren't dining from the King's table? Think of all the addictions our society struggles with such as drugs, alcohol, food, shopping, sexual behaviors, gambling, relationships, approval of others at all costs, and a host of others. People look to a substance or behavior or an event in order to meet the cravings of their appetites, but none of those things fully satisfy. A drug addict doesn't become addicted because his drug of choice meets his need. Read what a former drug addict says of his experience: *"Due to feelings of inadequacy, inferiority, and fear of rejection, I never felt confident enough to talk to people I did not know or to even be real with the ones I did. The night I discovered cocaine I thought all of that changed. The drug gave me the illusion of security and because of that false security I felt the illusion of significance as well. However, as my use progressed, I found I needed more and more to reach the desired effect and later discovered that no amount would give me what I was looking for. It took 4 years for me to see the illusion for what it was and by then my life was nearly destroyed."* Those are the words of my very own husband, Stephen, speaking of his own life experiences. Other addictions work in much the same way. What we compromise in bringing into our lives thinking it will fill the void—thinking we get to be in control—eventually controls us, and if not dealt with in time, can destroy us. (We'll study more about this us in a later chapter.)

When we aren't going to God to meet our need for security and significance, the consequences are *always* painful—maybe not right away, but there is a pay day someday, and it eventually catches up to us all. It's interesting to note that this "dirt diet" is often noticed in young children, toddlers and younger. It's interesting to me to draw the parallel that a young, immature human being will settle for dirt, and even crave it, until they are mature enough to realize there are much healthier, and more enjoyable ways to feed that craving. Sometimes, most of the time actually, it takes a more mature person who genuinely cares for the child, to teach them to eat food rather than munching on dirt. God created wonderful ways to meet our needs that He has placed within us. And as we grow in maturity as a believer, we will find that there is nothing that will satisfy our longings more than what we can find in Him alone. No longer settling for "spiritual dirt", we can feast on what God has provided for us. And, then, as we mature, we can pass this knowledge onto others who are still settling for dirt, lovingly pointing them to what their heart is truly craving.

That being said, just like King Ahasuerus, who had it all by the world's standards –fame, wealth, power, women, and more—and yet remained unsatisfied, we often find ourselves spinning our own wheels trying to fill our own needs our way rather than God's perfect way. We often lose sight of the fact that God is FOR us. For those of us who know Him through a relationship with Jesus Christ, we need to honestly assess our trust in Him. We trusted Him to save us, but can we trust Him enough to obey Him today? If you're struggling to trust Him, tell Him. (He knows it already, by the way.) He can handle your honesty.

Take a few minutes to answer this question, "How are you seeking to fill your God-given needs for security and significance your way? What is the "dirt" you've been settling for?" Are you willing to step to the next level in the area of trust? We'll never trust perfectly this side of heaven, but we can grow in maturity in this area if we'll just be willing enough to take one step at a time. And as we do, we will find that we just don't crave the "dirt" anymore and that nothing satisfies us apart from the provisions found in our relationship with God Almighty.

Prayer: "Dearest Father, Thank you for your goodness to me in giving me the drive to feel both secure and significant. Show me where I am trying to fill these needs through any source other than from You. Just as physical hunger drives me to food so that I will be nourished, and thirst drives me to water so I can be satisfied, use my need for security and significance to drive me to You."

Going Deeper to Understand My Purpose:

1. Read John 4—the account of Jesus and the Samaritan Woman.

   A. Why do you suppose she was going to the well at the hottest part of the day?

   B. Jesus told her that He could offer her "living water". What was she using to satisfy her thirst for relationship?

   C. What did Jesus reveal to her would quench that thirst completely?

   D. Why do you suppose Jesus said that he "must go through Samaria"—keep in mind, Jews did NOT simply go through Samaria. Samaria was considered to be an unclean, unacceptable place for a Jew.

2. What did the Samaritan woman do with her jar after meeting Jesus?

   A. As we consider our own needs for security and significance, what "well" do you find yourself going to time after time, and what "jar" do you use to try to meet those needs?

B. Are you ready to trust God with those needs?

CHAPTER 2

It's My Party and I'll Divorce My Wife If I Want To! **(Part 2)**

❦

Esther 1:8-22

"⁸And drinking was according to the law; no one was compelled to drink, for the king had directed all the officials of his palace to serve only as each guest desired. ⁹Also Queen Vashti gave a banquet for the women in the royal house which belonged to King Ahasuerus. ¹⁰On the seventh day, when the king's heart was merry with wine, he commanded Mehuman, Biztha, Harbona, Bigtha, Abagtha, Zethar, and Carkas, the seven eunuchs who ministered to King Ahasuerus as attendants, ¹¹To bring Queen Vashti before the king, with her royal crown, to show the peoples and the princes her beauty, for she was fair to behold. ¹²But Queen Vashti refused to come at the king's command conveyed by the eunuchs. Therefore the king was enraged, and his anger burned within him. [13]Then the king spoke to the wise men who knew the times--for this was the king's procedure toward all who were familiar with law and judgment-- [14]Those next to him being Carshena, Shethar, Admatha, Tarshish, Meres, Marsena, and Memucan, the seven princes of Persia and Media who were in the king's presence and held first place in the kingdom. [15][He said] According to the law, what is to be done to Queen Vashti because she has not done the bidding of King Ahasuerus conveyed by the eunuchs? [16]And Memucan answered before the king and the princes, Vashti the queen has not only done wrong to the king but also to all the princes and to all the peoples who are in all the provinces of King Ahasuerus. [17]For this deed of the queen will become known to all women, making their husbands contemptible in their eyes, since they will say, King Ahasuerus commanded Queen Vashti to be brought before him, but she did not come. [18]This very day the ladies of Persia and Media who have heard of the queen's behavior will be telling it to all the king's princes. So contempt and wrath in plenty will arise. [19]If it pleases the king, let a royal command go forth from him and let it be written among the laws of the Persians and Medes, so that it may not be changed, that Vashti is to [be divorced and] come no more before King Ahasuerus; and let the king give her royal position to another who is better than she. [20]So when the king's decree is made and proclaimed throughout all his kingdom, extensive as it is, all wives will give honor to their husbands, high and low. [21]This advice pleased the king and the princes, and the king did what Memucan proposed. [22]He sent letters to all the royal provinces, to each in its own script and to every people in their own language, saying that every man should rule in his own house and speak there in the language of his own people. [If he had foreign wives, let them learn his language.]"

It is interesting that as stated in the beginning of this passage that no one was compelled to drink, so if someone should get drunk the fault was his own. But, after several months of this kind of daily and nightly activity, one cannot help but be affected, as we observe in this story. Day after day and night after night, month after month, and yet the king was still not satisfied with the affirmation he was receiving. After all these months, he has to go further to feel the same thing he felt on the first day of the party. (Remember what we discussed in Chapter 1?) Sin always follows this dark path. When we strive to meet our needs in our own way rather than God's way, we'll always be left wanting. It was no longer enough for the king to show off jewels and art and money. The only "possession" he had thus far kept unseen was his bride. Vashti was known for her beauty and the king, in his drunkenness, asked her to come to his party decked out and ready to wow his audience. THIS, he is certain, will make him feel like a man of power and prestige; THIS will make others revere him in a whole new way; surely THIS will fill his need and bring him satisfaction. No one was compelled to drink, and yet the king himself was drunk when he made the order to have Vashti come in and impress all the men with her beauty. This was the wrong thing for the king to do for several reasons.

First, the culture and law of that day did not allow for co-ed parties. It was just not done. Men partied and associated publicly with other men, and women with women. Vashti was entertaining her own guests when the request came, and she had to be shocked that the king would ask this of her. No self-respecting woman was going to walk into a room full of drunken men, especially when the obvious motive was to show off her beauty. What could she expect would happen to her as the only woman in a room full of drunken men?

In addition, Ahasuerus left himself open for refusal since the law was on her side. As a husband, it was his responsibility to protect his wife and her modesty, not to expose her to a bunch of drunken men. How unsafe this would be for a woman to do, much less for a queen who was to be kept from all men other than appointed eunuchs who would guard her husband's line of descendants. What must her husband have been thinking?! She openly refused his request.

Unfortunately for her, Vashti's decision ended very badly for her. The king was completely humiliated in front of all the guests he was trying so desperately to impress. Whatever her motive for continuing to refuse her husband's request — which was more importantly her king's command — it was seen as an unforgivable act. The queen held much influence over other women in the kingdom and the king and his advisors knew that other women would be impacted by this queen's decision. Could she have handled this in some other way? There is no evidence that she asked anyone for advice on the matter. In contrast to Esther, as we'll see in a later chapter, the queen went with what seemed humanly prudent to do, and it brought about her downfall.

As queen, she was still subject to her king. The impression is given and several commentators agree that Vashti defiantly refused to obey the king's order. To show up at his party would not have been unlawful, or sinful, but whatever her reasoning, she didn't have the foresight to realize how much this decision would cost her.

As a woman, I need to recognize that I have influence; maybe not as much as Vashti, but my choices and my behaviors do affect others around me. Just as Vashti's life and choices influenced the women of her day — good or bad — so it goes with my life as well.

Because of this decision, Vashti was removed from her royal position; she lost everything. The men who offered counsel to the king were very interested in remaining "kings" in their own homes and they greatly feared this decision made by the queen. Vashti had no idea what this seemingly "common sense" decision would cost her. I also need to be careful how I choose to respond to life's demands so that I do not lose my position.

So, how do I do this?

Through the study of God's Word and a willing heart to obey it.

The main way that God speaks to us is through His Word. Scripture says that God has elevated His word even above His Name.

Psalm 138:2 *"I will worship toward Your holy temple, And praise Your name For Your loving-kindness and Your truth; For You have magnified Your word above all Your name." NKJV*

If our reading and study of Scripture is merely to check off our daily list of good deeds, its power in our lives will be minimal. But, if we can get past that motivation and become motivated out of our deep romance with the One who wrote the love letter to us, it changes the whole thing. Just like any other meaningful, significant relationship, it doesn't happen by itself, and it doesn't happen overnight. It takes time and commitment from both involved. God has done and continues to do His part; I get to respond to Him. He has initiated the whole thing; I simply accept His gift of relationship through Christ's atonement on the Cross.

There was a time when I was a teenager that my church was beginning to experience a lot of growth, both in numbers and depth of relationship with God. During those early days of growth, under the leadership of our very dynamic leader, many people became quite interested in learning more about the occult in order to be better equipped to handle those false teachings. Well, I wanted to be knowledgeable too, so I started reading about witchcraft, black magic, and the rest. Rather than be informed and prepared, I was becoming fearful and intimidated. Then one day Pastor Johnny talked about how the Bible needs to have the preeminence in our lives above any other books we might be reading. Christian literature definitely has its place and I am an avid reader, but the Bible must come first. He gave the illustration that you may be familiar with, but it makes a very good point. He said that when bankers are being trained, those who are training them do not bring them every counterfeit they can find in order for the bankers to know all of the counterfeits that may or may not come their way. Think about it; they would have to be trained daily because counterfeits are constantly being manufactured. Rather, they are trained to memorize the real deal—that way, whenever a fake comes across their desk, they can spot it immediately! Realizing the wisdom of that, I began to really delve into the Bible, and I can honestly say that putting Scripture to memory has guarded me from false teachings on many, many occasions. I don't have to rely on someone else's relationship with God, I have my own!

Through prayer that is intimate and responsive to the Lord's voice.

First, if we can learn to trust God enough with who we really are—the good, the bad, and the ugly, and be ourselves completely when we pray, we are going to see walls come down that are hindering and blocking the intimacy God desires for us to have with Him. Russell Willingham says something in <u>Relational Masks</u> that has really stayed with me. He said, "When we take an honest look at ourselves, it really is as bad as we thought it was, (in fact, it's worse!). " He goes on to explain that that is where God's grace comes in and does its work in our lives. God's grace changes us most when we're honest about who we really are, when we're honest about our own brokenness, rather than using our energy and resources to put up a false image based on what we would rather believe about ourselves.

The perfect pattern for prayer can be found in Scripture as we look to Jesus as our example. Throughout the Gospels, we read about Jesus praying. His disciples asked Him to teach them how to pray—and He did! (See Matthew 6; Mark 11 and 12; Luke 11:1-13) Jesus taught them that first they need to have a place and time to pray. If we want to have impact through our prayers, then we must develop the discipline of prayer. Yes, there are also verses that tell us to pray always, without ceasing, and we can talk to God whenever we need to, but our level of intimacy with the Father will reflect much and be developed in our times of prayer and aloneness with Him. I can call my husband on his cell phone pretty much whenever I want to and say what's on my mind quick and fast, but intimacy comes from time alone, unhurried, where both of us have time to speak and to share and to be heard.

Then when we pray we need to recognize and acknow-ledge God for Whom He is. Prayer that will be effective will be the prayer that is spoken in honesty and surrender. As I worship God for Whom He is, (holy, all-knowing, all-powerful, good, righteous, perfect, just, amazing, omni-present, loving, grace-full, merciful---the list could go on and on forever!), I begin to see Him as I need to see Him and I also recognize my complete dependency on Him for everything.

Jesus also taught his disciples to pray for God's will to be done on earth (i.e. in my life) as it is in Heaven. He taught them to pray for their needs to be met, recognizing that God is the Provider of all our needs. He taught them to pray for relationships—to forgive as we forgive. God is the ultimate authority on the subject of forgiveness, and it's His grace that will enable us to forgive. He taught us to pray God's protection over our lives from temptation and from the evil one. And He concludes the "Lord's Prayer/Disciple's Prayer" where He began—giving glory to the Father.

Simply going through the motions of the Christian life isn't going to bring us into victorious living even if we follow the patterns and rules perfectly (which we're powerless to do). I must get to know the God who has done everything to get to know me, so that I can learn what it means to allow Him to live His life through me. I often hear people say, "Shelley, I'm not like you--*I just can't hear from God*." I remember believing that same thing. I would see others who seemed to have such a deep connection and closeness with God and it seemed unattainable *for me*. But, I was determined that if it was even slightly possible, I wanted to know God like that, too. And, I have come to realize that as James, the half-brother of Jesus wrote, when we draw near to God, He indeed draws near to us.

It's like a phone call—if my mom calls me, she doesn't have to identify herself. I know her voice. I have heard her voice for so long, that now it is very distinguishable to me. But if someone I'm not as familiar with calls me, I might not know right away who it is unless he/she identifies him/herself. The more time I spend with someone, the more I recognize the voice. And, the same holds true for God. In the beginning, you might not be so sure you're hearing Him, but as you walk with Him in relationship rather than rigid religion, which is all about what you do, not who God has made you to be, your ears will become tuned to the Voice of their Maker. It is worth what it takes to get there!

Prayer is communication, and communication is not a one-sided deal. Notice that prayer is not simply about talking to God which is what many, if not most, believe it to be. Prayer is also more importantly about *listening to* God. Sometimes His silence can be deafening, but as we wait on Him, and as we make the decision to be disciplined enough to listen for His voice, we'll begin to notice that He isn't as silent as we once believed. More times than not, His silence is not silence at all; it's just that His voice has been crowded out by all the other "noise" in our lives. Have you ever been to a music concert where you could hear nothing but the sounds from the speakers? Have you ever thought about trying to have a personal conversation during those events? Probably not, right? And yet how often do our lives consist of our doing all the talking when it comes to prayer? God's voice is totally drowned out by all the other competing noises in our lives. There is a very worthwhile discipline of learning to listen and making the effort to allow ourselves to actually hear the *Still, Small Voice* of our Holy God. He longs for us to recognize His voice and for us to make the time to hear from Him.

For the times when He chooses to give us the gift of His silence, (yes, I said "gift"), it may be that He is doing a very significant work in our lives to bring us to greater maturity and strength in our walk as a believer. It's often in the times of God's silence that we learn and grow the most. We are forced in these times to live out what we already know to be true without requiring some new revelation or word from God. I can attest to the reality that these times are never times where God is absent, although it can feel that way. And I can also testify that these times are worth it — don't waste what God is allowing you to experience. And, when the time comes, and you receive a fresh word from God, it makes all the days of silence completely worth it!

By getting counsel from those who are walking closely with the Lord.

In Proverbs, we're told several times that plans fail for a lack of counsel and that in the multitude of counselors, there is safety. There must be a balance, though: we must not simply run to our girlfriends and get advice. We must avoid the temptation to go only to the people we know will tell us what we want to hear. Sometimes the most valuable advice I receive is the advice most difficult to accept. We must be wise about whom we go to for Godly counsel. Sometimes the very best counsel is the opposite of what we'd like to hear, but coming from a man or woman who walks with God in integrity and allows the Lord to reign in his/her life, we can take their words very seriously, recognizing the preciousness of earnest, heartfelt counsel.

There are different kinds of relationships given to us for different purposes. For example, some people in my life are *advisors*. These are people I know to be people of integrity, Godly wisdom, and sound doctrine. I don't go to them to find a shoulder to cry on, I go to them to receive counsel on decision-making. Other people are *accountability partners*. These are women who know me up close and personal, women who are growing in their relationship with the Lord; we are women who believe in getting below the surface most relationships offer in order to help each other reach our potential in Christ. And, lastly, other relationships are those close friendships that are developed over time. These are the people I can call day or night and know that they will love and accept me no matter what. I call these relationships *authentic friendships*.

God has given us amazing resources in His Word, through prayer, and in relationships with other believers. Take advantage of everything He has made available to you!

Don't settle for mediocre, just-getting-by Christianity. The abundant life awaits you…go after it!!

Prayer: "Lord, where do I have influence? Am I allowing You to use my influence for Your will or for my own agenda?"

Going Deeper to Understand My Purpose:

1. Spend some time today praying—just be yourself and talk to the One who is waiting to hear from you today. Take time to be still before your Heavenly Father and listen to what He is saying. Write down the things that come to your mind. What are the areas of your life that He is dealing with? What is your response to Him?

2. Read the following verses on prayer and then ask the Lord what He is saying directly to you today. As you journal your journey with the Lord, you will be blessed as you look back to this time of growth. I highly recommend journaling if you haven't already started doing this.

   A. *Luke 18:1*

   B. *Romans 12:12*

C. *Ephesians 6:18*

D. *Colossians 4:2*

E. *Matthew 6:6*

3. Ask the Lord to make you aware of people in your life to whom He would have you invest time in getting to know—people of wisdom who you know you could go to in order to obtain wise counsel that will be Biblically balanced. Who are those people? (Don't let your heart get discouraged if you don't think of several names right now. Just continue to pray for the Lord's provision of this; and allow Him to make YOU that kind of person for someone else.)

CHAPTER 3

On Purpose For a Purpose
Esther 2:1-8

❧

"1AFTER THESE things, when the wrath of King Ahasuerus was pacified, he [earnestly] remembered Vashti and what she had done and what was decreed against her. 2Then the king's servants who ministered to him said, Let beautiful young virgins be sought for the king. 3And let the king appoint officers in all the provinces of his kingdom to gather all the beautiful young virgins to the capital in Shushan, to the harem under the custody of Hegai, the king's eunuch, who is in charge of the women; and let their things for purification be given them. 4And let the maiden who pleases the king be queen instead of Vashti. This pleased the king, and he did so. 5There was a certain Jew in the capital in Shushan whose name was Mordecai son of Jair, the son of Shimei, the son of Kish, a Benjamite, 6Who had been carried away from Jerusalem with the captives taken away with Jeconiah king of Judah, whom Nebuchadnezzar the king of Babylon had carried into exile. 7He had brought up Hadassah, that is Esther, his uncle's daughter, for she had neither father nor mother. The maiden was beautiful and lovely, and when her father and mother died, Mordecai took her as his own daughter. 8So when the king's command and his decree were proclaimed and when many maidens were gathered in Shushan the capital under the custody of Hegai, Esther also was taken to the king's house into the custody of Hegai, keeper of the women."

I am so excited to get to this chapter! We finally get to the lives of Esther and Mordecai. These are two people I would have loved to have known; to be able to observe their relationship with one another; and to have spoken with them. For the believer, we know that our lives are eternal ones, and because of this reality, I can say with excitement that these are two individuals I look forward to meeting one day in Heaven.

God's sovereignty is seen throughout this story. Long before the plot to kill the Jews is introduced, God uses all things to bring about His divine plan. This has huge impact for us today. If we will truly grasp the fact that God is absolutely in charge, we would trust Him more—even when things do not make sense from our vantage point. Not only did God use the sinful and ugly relationship issues between King Ahasuerus and Queen Vashti, God used the hardships of Esther's life to bring her to this point in history. He truly does use "*all* things *together* for our good" (Romans 8:28,emphasis mine).

In this chapter, we'll look at some interesting aspects to Esther's life that also apply to our own. This is a young woman who comes onto the scene of history at a crucial time. Long before she was born the Jews had been taken into Babylonian captivity as a result of their own continued disobedience. God had warned His people of the judgment that would come if they continued to rebel against Him. He is not a man that He should lie, and when the Jews by and large continued to be hard-hearted against Him, He fulfilled His warnings. The final captivity occurred about 100 years before the time of Esther, in 586 BC. During those 100 years, God's mercy was extended to His people as He sovereignly moved on the hearts of pagan kings to show kindness to the Jews in releasing them from captivity and allowing them to return home to rebuild the Temple of God. This, too, fulfilled God's prophecy through Jeremiah that the captivity would last 70 years. God's discipline came as a necessary tool to bring the hearts of His people back to Him.

During the first return, a Godly man named Zerubbabel led those who chose to return to begin rebuilding the Temple. Ezra came on the scene later to finish the job. (*You can read more about this in the book of Ezra in the Old Testament.*) It was supremely important that God's Temple be built so that God's people would have a place to worship and to deal with their sins. They did not have the New Covenant made possible through Christ's sacrifice, and therefore, did not have God's Spirit living inside of them. In order to have the honor of being in right fellowship with God, they *had* to have a place, the Temple, to offer the sacrifices required to deal with their sin. God's holiness requires extreme specifications to allow humanity into His perfect presence. His justice demands payment be made for sin. Today it might be difficult to understand the importance of rebuilding the Temple, because as Christians under the New Covenant, we *are* the Temple of the Holy Spirit. We no longer have to offer animal sacrifices because God Himself provided the ultimate sacrifice on our behalf when He sent His only Son to die for our sins. It is no longer necessary for us to have a building made of hands for God to dwell in among us; we are the place of His habitation. Amazing!! For people living before Christ's death, however, having the Temple was paramount.

Approximately 50,000 Jews followed Zerubbabel when he led the return. Others went with Ezra when he returned. There were, however, many Jews who remained, choosing not to return to Jerusalem. Esther, whose name in Hebrew is actually Hadasseh, was part of the remnant that remained; and as the title of this study and this chapter suggest, this too was part of God's overall, sovereign purpose for His people.

The time in history in which she was born

It was not by chance that Esther was born during this crucial time in history. It was not by some cosmic coincidence that Esther just happened to be born when she was born. God had her in mind from the very foundation of the world, and He had a specific plan designed with her in mind.

If we can all embrace the reality that God has us right here, right now *on purpose*, *for a purpose*, it will change our entire outlook on life. It will impact our relationships, our goals, and events we experience—both positive and negative. God is writing an amazing story and each of us holds an irreplaceable role in that story.

Oh, how the culture of our day would be impacted if people could accept that God has a good purpose for each and every life! I have miscarried four times and I can honestly tell you that although I don't know every purpose those four babies had for their short time in my womb and in my life, I do see purpose for their lives. God creates no one He doesn't also have a purpose for, and there are no accidents (no matter what you've been told); *there are no less important or less significant lives in God's sight*. What makes the difference is our own perspective—do we believe God, or do we believe the lies of our day?

My oldest child, Amelia, was telling me recently about a boy in her school who does not believe people are born with purpose. He believes we're simply born, live our lives, and die.

No more, no less. I was impressed with how she responded to him. She told him that she makes her little brother's lunch for him every day (and this mom is so thankful!). She said, "What if my only purpose was to see to it that my little brother has a lunch to eat? That little thing is important, and all by itself, it serves a purpose." I am so thankful that even at her young age of twelve years, she has begun to realize that God has placed us where He has on purpose for a purpose.

When I was a young girl, my favorite show on TV and my favorite books to read were the Little House on the Prairie shows and books. I would spend hours pretending I lived back then and would drive my family crazy with all my "yes'm's" and walking like I was blind (like Mary). I lived in a fantasy that I would be transported back in time where I would be appreciated for who I was, I would be everyone's best friend, I would go to the pond and fish or swim and I would just be "happy". I truly believed at 9 years of age that if I had only been born back then, that I would have been happier; and that somehow, God made a mistake in allowing me to born in 1974. Surely, I was about 100 years overdue! My mom snapped me into reality one day when she told me the cold, hard truth that I wouldn't be so happy living in a world with no deodorant, no blow dryers for my hair, and having to kill dinner before we could eat it! I hate it when Mom is right!

There are parents and grandparents who have said that they wish their children and grandchildren could enjoy the world in which they grew up. A time when crime wasn't so rampant, when the biggest problems in the public schools were gum chewing and leaving trash on the floors. It's important to remember, that although there have been seasons where life might have appeared simpler and better, there has never been a time in history in which people didn't need a savior. There has never been a time so wonderful that there wasn't pain, sorrow, abuse, crime, and death. It's important for us to remember that ever since the fall of man in the Garden of Eden, there has been danger for all of mankind.

You may not have had those same daydreams that I had about getting to be part of the "Ingall's" family, but have you ever wondered if your life is really as purposeful or meaningful as it *could have been* had you been born in some other time in history; if you could have been born somewhere besides where you were born; when things were simpler, better, happier—or a place where things seemed better? As my mom pointed out to me, there is no perfect time in history outside of the Garden of Eden—everything else falls so short. So, my friend, I have something to tell you: You were born on exactly the right and perfect date for your part in God's story! There was NO better time for Esther to be born, and there was no other time in history for you. Your birthday was divinely chosen by a God who is crazy about you and has some wonderful plans for you. So celebrate that birthday, no matter how many of them you've had. Your birthday was chosen as a gift from Almighty God and it's so important that you are here!

The family into which she was born

One of the biggest issues for most of us is how to deal with those who are closest to us in relationship—our families. Many of us feel totally out of place within our own homes. Some have felt this way since childhood, a feeling of just not fitting in for one reason or another—or for *many* reasons. I have actually been surprised by the number of women, of all ages, who have shared this feeling.

Life is not fair. We all know this to be true and we'll even say it when we're being gut level honest. Sometimes the "spiritual" thing to say is something about how God uses everything for our good, but we say it hoping that it is true, not relying on it as absolute truth. Let's face it: some children *are* born into homes with adoring, loving parents committed to God and to one another. They lavish love and grace upon their children and there is a sense of acceptance that allows for growth, dreams and opportunities. Unfortunately, those kinds of homes are the exception rather than the rule.

For most of us, the dysfunction that comes from living in a sin-cursed world impacted us from very early on. I've done a lot of studying and learning about the different results that happen when children are brought up in dysfunctional homes. Satan loves an easy target—he doesn't care if you're only a child. He will do whatever he can to steal, kill and destroy. (See John 10:10. We'll discuss this in greater length in a later chapter.) And, often his ammo of choice is the sinful patterns by those we are the most vulnerable to—our family of origin. For some, the level of dysfunction is overwhelming. The word itself can sound so inadequate for the conditions that some children have had to endure. My heart aches when I hear of the violence and abuse that takes place in some families. It is overwhelming. How do we reconcile that God is good when He allows these horrible atrocities to take place right under His divine nose? I can't pretend to have all the answers, but I can say that as I have watched Him bring healing and purpose to the pain of abuse, I am amazed at His ability to bring incredible beauty out from the most gruesome ashes. He is God and He is good. Joni Eareckson Tada, in her memoir, <u>The God I Love</u> said, "Sometimes God allows the very thing He hates in order to bring about the very thing He loves." I also love what I heard Pastor Rick Warren of Saddleback Community Church, and author of <u>The Purpose Driven Life</u>, say recently in an interview on national TV. He said something to this effect: "God knew the exact DNA that was needed for each person to be born; there are accidental parents, but never an accidental person." Even the people with the ugliest family situations were designed on purpose by a loving Creator with a very important purpose for their lives.

Esther's biological family was chosen by God—on purpose, for a purpose. There must have been times when she questioned God's decision to put her into the family in which He did. Why couldn't she have been born to a nice Jewish family who wasn't living in exile? Why did He choose *this* family? It was by no mistake that *her* parents were married, conceived, and gave birth to her. It was not by some weird coincidence that they had young "Hadasseh". God had something very special in mind and He had been planning to use her in a significant way since before time began. He has done the same for each one of us. Hard to believe, isn't it? Believing truth doesn't make it truth though, does it? Truth is truth, regardless of what we think about it or how we feel about it.

The death of her parents

If it wasn't bad enough that the Jews were in captivity, somehow—and we don't know how—and at some point, Esther's parents died and left her orphaned. This, too, was part of God's providential plan in the story He was writing. Bad things often happen to good people—to *God's people*. And when these things occur, we're often left wondering, "Can God really be trusted? Is He really who He says He is? If God is so good, then why has He allowed _____ to happen?" I've struggled with these very questions myself. I mean, why on earth would a loving God allow this poor young girl to be orphaned? What "greater purpose" could there be? In the moment of suffering, in the season of suffering, it is often very difficult to even imagine anything good or beautiful coming from such a tragedy. Innocent people are dealt horrific blows every single day and, as mentioned earlier, we are often left wondering how a good and loving God can allow this. I don't presume to have all the answers to all the "why" questions, but I do have some grasp on the fact that God sees the end from the beginning. There are experiences I've had to walk through and hated having to go through them, only to come out on the other side thanking God for those very experiences because of the depth of relationship I gained with Him as a result.

James 5:10-11 says, "10 My brethren, take the prophets, who spoke in the name of the Lord, as an example of suffering and patience. 11 Indeed we count them blessed who endure. You have heard of the perseverance of Job and **seen the end intended by the Lord**—that the Lord is very compassionate and merciful." (NKJV; emphasis mine)

There is an "end intended of the Lord" in each of our lives! This gives me hope and comfort when the pain seems too much to bear.

Our pain is on purpose, for a purpose, my friend. God won't explain it all to us, He doesn't need to. When we're willing to walk through anything with Him and for Him, we come to find we no longer need to have every question answered. It's a process of intimacy that doesn't happen quickly, but if we will make the choice to persevere, we will come to a place where we can truly say "All to Jesus, I surrender, All to Him I freely give."

The availability of Mordecai to raise her

We find, in the life and story of Mordecai that not only was Esther created on purpose, for a purpose, but the same was true for Mordecai (if you haven't figured it out by now, I'm making the point that we ALL are created on purpose for a purpose—smile). He was her close relative, possibly a cousin, who adopted her when her parents died. God, in His sovereignty, placed these two individuals into one another's lives because He had a purpose that involved the two of them being in authentic relationship with one another. These two people were building a trusting relationship with one another that God would soon use to rescue an entire nation! Amazing!

Mordecai was available to obey God—are you? God planned all of Mordecai's life to prepare him for this time as well. God was sovereign over all the things that had to take place—*his* time in history, his parents, his pain, etc. And the same goes for everyone before him. We are not subject to chance and luck. We have access to God, the Creator, who holds ALL things in His hands! In studying other commentaries and writings on this book of Scripture, I came across a well-known commentator who makes the claim that Mordecai was out of God's will because he was still living in Persia instead of having returned to Israel when he had the chance. I disagree with much of this commentator's opinions on this matter based on how this story unfolds and how Mordecai responded, but, even if the commentator is correct, it doesn't change the point I'm making in this study: God uses all things to bring about His good will, even our own mistakes and shortcomings. Friend, no matter what has happened in your past, you are never so far gone that God's grace can't work in your life. I personally believe that Mordecai was a man of faith and trusted God, imperfectly as we all do, and that the Lord had him right where He wanted him to fulfill the purpose he was created to accomplish.

The final thought I want to express is this: not only does God use ALL of the pain we experience; He also uses the good things as well. "All things" means just what it says: *all* things. God uses all things together, and only He is sovereign enough to know what mixture of circumstances, DNA, relationships, experiences, etc. will work together to bring about His intended end in each of our lives. This understanding can make a world of difference in how we respond to life's positive blessings as well as how we respond when others are blessed in a way we may not be. God is working in each of our lives individually and corporately at the same time. Let Him have His way—you can trust Him!

Prayer: "Father, thank you for making me and everything about me on purpose, for a purpose. Help me to live this out, even when I don't fully believe all of it yet, or understand what it all means."

Going Deeper to Understand My Purpose:

1. Romans 8:28 says that "God works all things together for good..."

   A. Do you simply believe/agree with this statement in your mind, or do you truly believe, down deep inside of you, that this is true for *you*?

   B. Answer in more depth as you consider the "in my mind" or "know this in my heart" question.

2. How do you imagine Esther felt about the fact that God had allowed her parents to die while other children still had their parents? Even if she never found herself able to express how she was impacted by their deaths, what would you imagine was deep down inside of her?

3. Have you ever thought about how you've been impacted by your own time in history, family of origin, etc? If so, describe what you've learned, if not, prayerfully ask the Lord to show you where you've believed the enemies lies.

4. In James 5:10-11, we read that we can look at the lives of others who have been blessed as they chose to endure great difficulty. Who is the greatest example of this in your life? Why? How has he/she impacted you? Share this with your small group.

5. We are told in Scripture to confess everything to God. Confession is simply agreeing with what God's Word says and telling it to God. Since He already knows it is there, confession isn't for Him—it's for us. Until we know and can admit what is inside of us, we can't fully accept the truth God has for us. Ask God to search your heart and reveal to you the hidden things that need to be dealt with by Him. Don't bother digging things up yourself, (His timing is perfect), but allow the Spirit of God to reveal areas in your life that need His touch.

CHAPTER 4

Purpose, Presence, Position

Esther 2:9-23

"9And the maiden pleased [Hegai] and obtained his favor. And he speedily gave her the things for her purification and her portion of food and the seven chosen maids to be given her from the king's palace; and he removed her and her maids to the best [apartment] in the harem. 10Esther had not made known her nationality or her kindred, for Mordecai had charged her not to do so. 11And Mordecai [who was an attendant in the king's court] walked every day before the court of the harem to learn how Esther was and what would become of her.

12Now when the turn of each maiden came to go in to King Ahasuerus, after the regulations for the women had been carried out for twelve months--since this was the regular period for their beauty treatments, six months with oil of myrrh and six months with sweet spices and perfumes and the things for the purifying of the women-- 13Then in this way the maiden came to the king: whatever she desired was given her to take with her from the harem into the king's palace. 14In the evening she went and next day she returned into the second harem in the custody of Shaashgaz, the king's eunuch who was in charge of the concubines. She came to the king no more unless the king delighted in her and she was called for by name.

15Now when the turn for Esther the daughter of Abihail, the uncle of Mordecai who had taken her as his own daughter, had come to go in to the king, she required nothing but what Hegai the king's attendant, the keeper of the women, suggested. And Esther won favor in the sight of all who saw her. 16So Esther was taken to King Ahasuerus into his royal palace in the tenth month, the month of Tebeth, in the seventh year of his reign. 17And the king loved Esther more than all the women, and she obtained grace and favor in his sight more than all the maidens, so that he set the royal crown on her head and made her queen instead of Vashti. 18Then the king gave a great feast for all his princes and his servants, Esther's feast; and he gave a holiday [or a lessening of taxes] to the provinces and gave gifts in keeping with the generosity of the king.

19And when the maidens were gathered together the second time, Mordecai was sitting at the king's gate. 20Now Esther had not yet revealed her nationality or her people, for she obeyed Mordecai's command to her [*to fear God and execute His commands] just as when she was being brought up by him. 21In those days, while Mordecai sat at the king's gate, two of the king's eunuchs, Bigthan and Teresh, of those who guarded the door, were angry and sought to lay hands on King

Ahasuerus. 22And this was known to Mordecai, who told it to Queen Esther, and Esther told the king in Mordecai's name. 23When it was investigated and found to be true, both men were hanged on the gallows. And it was recorded in the Book of the Chronicles in the king's presence." (AMP.)

The name of God is not mentioned in the original Hebrew text.

In this chapter we will look at three aspects to Esther and Mordecai's lives. These are three elements that I believe God wants to endow on each of us, albeit it won't ever look exactly the same in any two lives. God created each one of us with a unique plan and design. He is a very personal God; and I am so thankful that He is.

First we see that they each had a Purpose

There is a song by "Caedmon's Call" and one of the lyrics goes like this, "And You know the plans that You have for me...and You can't plan the ends and not plan the means...". ("40 Acres", 1999) That goes through my mind so often because it is so true; and because it is true, it encourages me. God knows the plans He has for me (Jeremiah 29:11) and they are GOOD plans. *He can't plan the ends without planning the means to get me to that end.* We *want* God to show us our purpose, we *want* to know our lives matter, but we struggle with what the Lord, in His infinite knowledge, knows it will take to get us there. In the book of Esther, and throughout Scripture, we get to see the means God uses to bring about His ends in the lives of those who have gone before us. It helps to build our faith and give us the confidence we need

to press on when we don't understand the "why's" to
His means.

In Esther 2:9, we see that Esther pleased Hegai, the
custodian of the women. Since he was a eunuch, he wasn't
pleased by her in an inappropriate way; this was a man very
accustomed to being around the most beautiful of women.
But there was something unique about Esther. The Lord
created her and instilled within her a personality that would
match with Hegai's—God's purposes prevail. We can trust
Him where He leads us. Everything about Esther was on
purpose and for a purpose bigger than herself—her looks,
her personality, her time in history, her IQ, her family, her
talents—*everything* was for a very significant purpose. God
has done the very same thing for me and for you. Everything
about you is on purpose, for a purpose. You already have
everything you need to accomplish what God wants to
accomplish through you today. WOW! Let that sink in for a
minute. You are lacking NOTHING you need to do exactly
what you need to do today. Don't worry about tomorrow...
God already has that under control. What I am learning more
and more as I grow in my relationship with God is that He
is interested in me *personally*: in loving me, in growing me,
in changing me, in helping me—and always in using me in
the lives of others in relationship. He has already given me
everything I need for Him to be able to do that within me and
through me.

II Peter 1:3-4:

*3 "For His divine power has given us everything
required for life and godliness, through the knowledge of Him who called us by His own glory and
goodness. 4 By these He has given us very great and
precious promises, so that through them you may*

share in the divine nature, escaping the corruption that is in the world because of evil desires."

(Holman Christian Standard Bible chosen for wording and translation purposes.)

As Esther submitted to God's will in the circumstances in which she was placed, she was blessed in her circumstances. We find that God didn't change her situation, but He blessed her in the place He put her. For example, she got to enjoy nicer food than what the other ladies received; she was given better beauty items; and she benefited by getting advice in friendship with Hegai. God will be good to us and if we're careful to acknowledge Him we'll see His goodness in our own lives even when He allows us to go through something that seems unfair or unloving. (Remember James 5:10-11.)

Mordecai was equally as significant to this whole story. His guidance was absolutely pivotal. Without Mordecai, this story would be completely different. Esther needed the godly wisdom of one who loved her and guided her. I, too, need godly counsel from others. I can't presume to do the work of God all alone. Esther's humility enabled her to continue to obey Mordecai even when she was no longer in his home and under his authority. She recognized the value of another person's advice; she remained teachable, a very important trait if we are going to grow and be used in a positive way.

Consider the wisdom of these verses found in Proverbs:

Proverbs 11:14
"Where there is no counsel, the people fall;
But in the multitude of counselors there is safety."

Proverbs 15:22
"Without counsel, plans go awry,
But in the multitude of counselors they are
established."

Proverbs 24:6
"For by wise counsel you will wage your own war,
And in a multitude of counselors there is safety."
(NKJV)

Mordecai obviously loved Esther in a very special way since he adopted her as his own child. Then we see that he paced back and forth as close to where she was every day so that he could find out how she was and to communicate through others with her. Mordecai delighted in Esther and deeply loved her. In what was possibly the biggest test of his faith, Mordecai did what any loving parent would do. Sometimes the most difficult things we face are the painful events that happen directly to our children or other loved ones, especially when we do not have any power to change the situation. Through it all, God was still in control! Picture Mordecai pacing back and forth, listening, and asking for any information on his beloved Esther, whose Persian name means "Star" — she was his star! What a special picture of God's love for us. He has adopted each of us who have accepted Him as Father through Jesus and longs to communicate with us regularly. And to Him, because of His character and grace, each of us is a "star" to Him. We each get to be his favorite, the apple of His eye! He never takes from one of His children to give to another. You, my friend, are loved more than you can possibly fathom. We have yet to grasp the amazing love and acceptance of God!

Next we find they had "Presence"

They were perfectly placed in the precise circumstances they were supposed to be in, even though they must have questioned God and themselves many times. Because of their willingness to submit to God's will during these times of great difficulty, they were able to be successful: **God's sovereignty guaranteed Esther success in her calling.** Verse 16 tells us that she came to live in the Palace. She and the other women went through many months of treatments. These days, women spend so much time, energy, and money on cosmetics, surgery, and beauty treatments. We see "reality" TV shows depicting the culture's drive for perfection and luxury. But none of this compares to what happened in the palace of King Ahasuerus. These girls got an *entire year* at the spa in order to be adequately prepared for their one night with the king. The pressure must have been unbelievable! The beauty treatments these ladies enjoyed were incredible, especially for their day. (I love to get my nails done or enjoy a massage, but I have never experienced in the *21st Century* what these young women enjoyed so many, many years ago. Try to imagine a WHOLE YEAR of spa treatments!) Then, after a full year of preparation: beauty classes, etiquette courses, classes on expectations of a Persian queen, and so on, she got her *one* shot with the king. This reminds me of the Olympics. Young athletes spend their entire lives, making sacrifice upon sacrifice, so that they can have that one shot at a gold medal. Everything up to that point is to prepare them to shine on this all-important, once-in-a-lifetime event. When the gold is won, it's got to be an incredible and even surreal moment. And then my mind goes to the ones who, for whatever reason, get out there, and blow it. Something that isn't supposed to happen happens, and the dream of going home a hero is gone. For some, next year brings a whole new opportunity; but not so for these ladies in a Persian harem. She could dress in whatever she wanted, she could take with her whatever she desired—this was her one and only opportunity to get the king's attention and affection. Can you imagine the nervousness of a young virgin? Talk about stress! How does one adequately prepare for such an expectation? She was expected—no, required—to be a *virgin*; unlike an athlete who gets to practice to make perfect; this young woman had to be completely inexperienced.

With that in mind, read verse 14b—*"She would not go in to the king again unless the king delighted in her and called for her by name."* (NKJV) If the king didn't like her enough, if she didn't measure up in the most intimate of situations, there was no hope for her. I feel such a sense of sadness when I read and imagine this. These were real people with real feelings, hopes, dreams…just like us. I can only imagine what these women went through days, weeks, months after that one solitary night with the king having never been called for again. This was never what God intended the wedding night to be! But, lost kings behave in ungodly ways, and I'm thankful that God can even use the godless acts of pagan kings to bring about His good will and purpose. That's how pagan kings operate.

I have a King and He knows me completely. Hebrews 4 teaches that I am already naked before Him—there is nothing hidden from Him—and yet, even with this complete knowledge of me, He loves and delights in me. This king doesn't demand, expect, or even desire that I come to offer Him what I hope or wish to be. He delights in my coming to Him just as I am. This king knows me more intimately than I even know myself. He knows everything there is to know about me, and my King doesn't use me and then forget me, as this pagan earthly king did to so many women. My King delights in me and calls me by my name!! WOW!! I don't have to manipulate or pretend with Him. If I do, He'll already know it anyway. What amazing hope this truth offers. Yes, the world offers pain, abuse, rejection, abandonment, but our hope is not in this world. Our hope is in the One True God, our King of kings!

We read in verse 17 that after the king saw her, the contest to find a queen was over. Esther became Queen in place of Vashti. I believe that Esther didn't just win the king's heart, but that she also gained his respect. I have a couple of reasons for coming to this conclusion.

Esther followed the advice given to her by someone who knew the king (Hegai), and because she was willing to follow guidance and the wisdom of others, she was rewarded with the crown and a banquet in her honor. She didn't presume to know everything as some of the other women did. She humbly sought the counsel of one who would know and then followed his advice.

I think her beauty was secondary to her strength and character from within. Think about it: rather than using all of the resources given to her on herself to gain attention and affirmation, she simply chose to concentrate more on the areas where God wants to develop character that would gain respect. What an example she is for us today! Rather than try to impress the king, she simply expressed to him who she really was. She walked in authenticity, and the king WAS impressed. In Proverbs 31, we read that physical charm and beauty is not lasting, and that true beauty shines from the inside out.

Proverbs 31 *"*²⁹*Many daughters have done virtuously, nobly, and well [with the strength of character that is steadfast in goodness], but you excel them all.* ³⁰*Charm and grace are deceptive, and beauty is vain [because it is not lasting], but a woman who reverently and worshipfully fears the Lord, she shall be praised!"* **(Amplified Bible)**

In verse 20, we see that Esther still chose to obey and respect Mordecai even after being crowned queen. She didn't forget who she was or become defiant and arrogant as Vashti did (in making decisions without consulting others). The king gave her a party and even named it for her. This king obviously liked to put on a good show, but this time, instead of giving himself a party, he honored his new queen with the "Feast of Esther". I wonder if he had learned something from how he treated Vashti perhaps.

Esther has set such a high standard, but not an unattainable one. She was simply who God created her to be. You can do that, and so can I, with the grace of God offered to us. So, my friend, even when you can't figure out what is going on, when God leads you somewhere, be ALL there!

God gave them Position

God put both Esther and Mordecai right where they needed to be, and gave them everything they needed to fulfill God's call on each of their lives, together and individually.

Mordecai was right where he needed to be when he overheard a plot to kill the king and then got word to Queen Esther (in her royal position) who in turn told the king. God made certain to provide Mordecai favor with the king long before he would need it. *Mordecai wasn't rewarded immediately.* But God saw and took note and made sure that the record was made so that when the day came that Mordecai would need to be recompensed for his faithfulness, he indeed would be. God puts each of us in the right place at the right time when we choose to walk with Him.

Sometimes God leads us to do things that seem meaningless to us when we do it, but it could be that He is giving us an opportunity to do right so that it can be for our good years later. Mordecai couldn't have known what was to come. He was faithful with what was entrusted to him, and grew in his abilities because of that. Before God gives us more, we need to be mature enough to handle with integrity and faithfulness that which He has already entrusted to us. When God sets the command to remain sexually pure, in our culture it can seem like such a harsh restriction, but God knows best and knows what awaits those who choose to go the way He has directed. When we are taught to tithe and trust God with our money as we give offerings, we can feel the "loss" of the immediate gratification (i.e. "if I tithe this income, I can't afford _____ _____ today"), but God is developing something within us that money cannot buy; a trust in Him that will amaze us if we'll allow Him to have His way according to His time table in our lives. Something money can't buy, but if it could, people would sell all, give all to attain the level of intimacy with their Creator that is available to each and every one of us who will make the choice to follow Him no matter what.

So, my friend, what is God saying to you today? Are you beginning to see that He has divinely ordered your life with a purpose in mind? We have so much to learn of our Heavenly Father and He faithfully waits for us to accept His invitation to know Him more.

> *Prayer: "Lord, thank you for Your sovereignty that I can fully rely upon and rest in. Thank you that I can walk in confidence in my calling because You are the One who holds the power to place me right where I am supposed to be when I am supposed to be there. Help me to trust You with my whole heart even when nothing makes sense to me."*

Going Deeper to Understand My Purpose

Here are a few words of wisdom to ponder:

When God calls us to do something, He will equip us and provide everything we need for that calling. *Kay Arthur* once said, "When God calls you, your only responsibility is to obey. It is not for you to try to make things happen. He will move Heaven and Earth to place you where you are supposed to be." (National Women's Conference, 2004)

"God's wisdom serves its own purposes by man's folly." *Matthew Henry Commentary,* referring to King Ahasuerus' decision to remove Vashti and hold a "beauty pageant" to find the new queen.

"Abraham didn't balk at the magnitude of the task, (sacrificing Isaac). God will always provide a way for you to do the thing He's called you to do, and often it won't be provided the way you saw coming. God will provide & He cherishes your obedient heart." *Chuck Allen, Benj Smith Extraordinary Leadership*

"...Apart from the clear call of God and our certain response to Him, we will influence people the wrong way. We must know our calling in order to have the correct influence on the correct people at the correct time." *Chuck Allen, Benj Smith Extraordinary Leadership*

Thank you for choosing to go further in your study. I pray it will bring blessing to your life as you get to know God better through His word.

As we study the Scriptures, I often think of the Apostle Paul and how much of his time as a believer was spent behind prison bars. There must have been times when he thought if only his circumstances could be different what more he could do for Christ's cause. I often think about the circumstances that we often struggle with in our time in history and in our culture;

i.e. "If I only made more money, then I could ....."; "If only my children were a little older, then I could ....."; "If only I could live _____, then I would feel.....''; "If only.... then....".

1. Notice that we often have these "If only, thens" without really realizing it. Allow yourself to be honest about these areas knowing that God is already aware and loves you right where you are. What are the "if only, thens" in your life?

2. Notice, too, that "only" is a deceptive word. For example, I often think "If only I made more money, then I could really bless the Church by what I could help support financially". What I've learned that really means is, "If only I made more money and could help the church more financially, I would feel like a more significant part of the Body of Christ; since I can't, I don't feel like what I have to offer makes me very important." God has had to show me this reality. There is nothing wrong with the desire to give more, but if I believe a lie in the midst of that desire, I am not walking in truth. The truth is that I have exactly, right now, TODAY, what God wants me to have and can do exactly what He has purposed for me today right where I am with the amount of money I have. How does this truth affect your "if only, thens"?

3. Read Philippians 4:11-13 from the Amplified Bible: *"11 Not that I am implying that I was in any personal want, for I have learned how to be content (satisfied to the point where I am not disturbed or disquieted) in whatever state I am. 12 I know how to be abased and live humbly in straitened circumstances, and I know also how to enjoy plenty and live in abundance. I have learned in any and all circumstances the secret of facing every situation, whether well-fed or going hungry, having a sufficiency and enough to spare or going without and being in want. 13 I have strength for all things in Christ Who empowers me [I am ready for anything and equal to anything through Him Who infuses inner strength into me; I am self-sufficient in Christ's sufficiency]."*

A. What does Scripture say about the Apostle Paul and his ability to be content?

B. What other Scriptures have you found that have helped you to trust in God's sovereignty over your situations & that have helped you to grow in the area of contentment? Share these with your small group.

4. What is the main thing you sense God saying to you in this section of study?

CHAPTER 5

Idolatry, Identity, and Impudence

Esther 3:1-13

"1AFTER THESE things, King Ahasuerus promoted Haman the son of Hammedatha the Agagite and advanced him and set his seat above all the princes who were with him. 2And all the king's servants who were at the king's gate bowed down and did reverence to Haman, for the king had so commanded concerning him. But Mordecai did not bow down or do him reverence. 3Then the king's servants who were at the king's gate said to Mordecai, Why do you transgress the king's command? 4Now when they spoke to him day after day and he paid no attention to them, they told Haman to see whether Mordecai's conduct would stand, for he had told them that he was a Jew. 5And when Haman saw that Mordecai did not bow down or do him reverence, he was very angry. 6But he scorned laying hands only on Mordecai. So since they had told him Mordecai's nationality, Haman sought to destroy all the Jews, the people of Mordecai, throughout the whole kingdom of Ahasuerus. 7In the first month, the month of Nisan, in the twelfth year of King Ahasuerus, Haman caused Pur, that is, lots, to be cast before him day after day [to find a lucky day for his venture], month after month, until the twelfth, the month of Adar. 8Then Haman said to King Ahasuerus, There is a certain people scattered abroad and dispersed among the peoples in all the provinces of your kingdom; their laws are different from every other people, neither do they keep the king's laws. Therefore it is not for the king's profit to tolerate them. 9If it pleases the king, let it be decreed that they be destroyed, and I will pay 10,000 talents of silver into the hands of those who have charge of the king's business, that it may be brought into the king's treasuries. 10And the king took his signet ring from his hand [with which to seal his letters by the king's authority] and gave it to Haman son of Hammedatha the Agagite, the Jews' enemy. 11And the king said to Haman, The silver is given to you, the people also, to do with them as it seems good to you. 12Then the king's secretaries were called in on the thirteenth day of the first month, and all that Haman had commanded was written to the king's chief rulers and to the governors who were over all the provinces and to the princes of each people, to every province in its own script and to each people in their own language; it was written in the name of King Ahasuerus and it was sealed with the king's [signet] ring. 13And letters were sent by special messengers to all the king's provinces--to destroy, to slay, and to do away with all Jews, both young and old, little children and women, in one day, the thirteenth day of the twelfth month, the month of Adar, and to seize their belongings as spoil." (Amplified Bible)

Welcome to Chapter 5 of studying the life of Esther and Mordecai; as we seek to learn how we were created "on purpose, for a purpose." I trust that the Lord is using this to encourage you that you are indeed made for a divine purpose that *only you* can fulfill.

With every person God has ever used in a historically significant way, there has also been an enemy or other great opposition to overcome. Here are just a few examples:

❖ David had Goliath

❖ Joseph had Potiphar's wife

❖ The three Hebrew boys and Daniel had their culture

❖ Jeremiah had the ungodly, unrepentant "religious" people

❖ Paul had his "thorn in the flesh"

…and the most beloved stories are the ones where the hero/heroine overcomes incredible and seemingly impossible odds.

We all prefer to watch the amazing stories unfold of great people overcoming great obstacles. Life (and books, and movies, and…) would be so mundane without the opposition. Think of how bored you'd be playing Ms. Pac-Man if she didn't have ghosts after her. Sure, it would be easier, but how boring!

If we are indeed going to allow God to have His way in our lives, we will come against opposition. Bank on it! A person only becomes as great as the opposition he/she overcomes. For Esther and Mordecai, there was Haman.

Idolatry

In Esther 3:1-2a we read that the king ordered all the people to bow and pay homage to Haman, an Amalekite. This is interesting because earlier in the Bible, we read that King Saul disobeyed God when he did not destroy these people—enemies of Israel. Anytime we choose to disobey God, others are negatively affected. Partial and/or delayed obedience equals disobedience and with it comes consequences for us and for others. Had Saul obeyed God's order to destroy this ungodly people group, enemies of God and the Israelites, we would never have heard of Haman, the Amalekite.

In ordering the Jewish people to bow to a man in this manner, Haman was really ordering them to show allegiance to himself, as though he was divine, which Jews were forbidden to do for anyone other than God.

Identity

In Esther 3:2b-4 we read that only one person chose not to go along with the status quo: Mordecai refused to bow. He is the only one mentioned for having refused. This astounds me, that of all the Jews living in that day, Mordecai is the only one with the courage to not bow. The people around are puzzled and ask him why he won't bow. Think about it—what was the big deal? Did it mean that in Mordecai's heart he was giving allegiance to Haman if he just went along with what everyone else was comfortable doing? Read that last sentence again and give pause to think about that statement. The world and even other believers will notice if I take a stand and will want to know "why?" too. Why don't I think we should allow homosexual marriage; why don't I think a mother should have the right to destroy her own unborn child; why don't I believe divorce should be

allowed for any and every reason; why do I believe in absti-
nence outside of marriage; why I am so intolerant as to
believe Jesus Christ is the ONLY way? We need to be ready
when they ask "WHY?" In 2 Timothy 2:15, the Bible says,
"[15]Study and be eager and do your utmost to present yourself to God approved (tested by trial), a workman who has
no cause to be ashamed, correctly analyzing and accurately
dividing [rightly handling and skillfully teaching] the Word
of Truth." (Amplified)

Mordecai knew who he was; he revealed his identity as
his reason for not bowing. He was a Jew and he had spent
enough time studying the Scriptures and walking with God
to know better than to sacrifice his integrity on the altar of
the culture of his day. Just because everyone else was doing
it, it didn't mean it was okay for him. He knew the principal
that says, "He who walks uprightly walks securely" Proverbs
10:9a. *It was safer for Mordecai to NOT bow than it was
TO bow.* In bowing he would have been going against God
Himself. He knew who he was; he was a Jew. **My understanding of my identity will determine what I will bow
to and what I will refuse to bow to**. If I understand that I
am a child of the Most High God, then that will make all the
difference in the choices and compromises I will or will not
make. That understanding is vital. And, as we'll see later on
in this study, Satan knows this as well, and will do whatever
he can to get us to be confused about this very foundational
truth.

Impudence *(Webster's defines this as "marked by contempt-
uous or cocky boldness or disregard of others")*

Finally, in Esther 3:5-13 we get some very interesting
plot points to this non-fictional story. Mordecai's actions
were reported to Haman and Haman got ticked! Haman was
arrogant and felt a sense of entitlement; who would dare to

refuse to bow to him, a man of greatness? Read Proverbs 16:18. I love how the Message translation reads: "[18]First pride, then the crash—the bigger the ego, the harder the fall." Haman's hatred was HUGE! He didn't just want revenge on Mordecai; he wanted all of Mordecai's people to be destroyed as well. There was a long standing discord between Jews and Amalekites, and this seemed to be the perfect solution to Haman to once and for all end the relationship with the enemies of his people. Just as Saul's disobedience yielded negative consequences for Israel, Mordecai's obedience SEEMINGLY does the same thing. If we stop reading at this point, we might be left to imagine that what Mordecai did wasn't worth it. We have to remember that God sees the end from the beginning and He has GOOD plans! (Refer again to Jeremiah 29:11; James 5:10-11.) The book of Proverbs is full of verses that speak of God's refuge for us when we'll be faithful to walk in His ways. It is important to remember that God is still sovereign even when we don't understand what He is up to, and when we don't sense His presence and protection in our lives. He will not leave us nor forsake us! (Deut. 31:6) Just think of the times in your life when you wanted something so badly, and were so upset when you didn't get what you wanted, only to be filled with gratitude down the road when you realized how good God was to keep you from what you *thought you wanted.*

God will use anyone who is willing to allow Him to have His way. He is about relationship, loving and blessing us and using that to love and bless others. But the flipside of this is also true. Satan will use anyone who is willing to allow HIM to have his way. He is about destruction; he will let us believe his ways are FOR us, but they are really about destroying us and others. Satan knew the Messiah was promised through the Jewish nation and therefore attempted many times to destroy them all.

Just as God uses our humility to prosper us, our descendants and our culture, Satan will use our own prideful arrogance to bring about his own plans of destroying us and as many others as he possibly can. God loves me, His grace is *for* me, and He wants to use my life to impact others for good. Satan hates me and wants to abuse me and use me to take down others.

The lot is cast and the king is deceived

Lots were cast in order to allow "chance" to decide when the attack would take place, but realize this. God is sovereign!! Nothing is by chance; nothing finds God off-guard. I'm sure by now you've probably heard the saying, "Has it ever occurred to you that nothing occurs to God?" We can see the sovereignty of God in other places in scripture when lots were cast. For example, in Jonah's story, when he was on the boat trying his best to leave behind God's presence and God's plan for him. The heathen sailors cast lots to find out who on the boat was the cause of the horrible storm. And, guess to whom the lots fell? Jonah of course! We also see God's sovereignty when lots were cast at the crucifixion of Christ, and men cast those lots to see who would win Jesus' robe. Throughout history, God has used man's best self-efforts and schemes to fulfill His own good plans. We can trust Him to take care of us. Proverbs says in Chapter 21:30 "There is no wisdom, no insight, no plan that can succeed against the Lord." (NIV) God is in control!

Getting back to Esther's story, we read that since the king trusted Haman he went along with his plans. Haman used manipulation and deception, *trying to make the king think this was in* the king's *best interest.*

In verse 10 Haman is referred to as 'the enemy of the Jews', revealing his true identity. Haman made himself his own god, looking to feed his hunger for security and significance his own way and in doing so, and without realizing it, he was really bowing to Satan. Our lives are far bigger than just us, far bigger than just what our eyes behold. Satan does the same thing in our lives when he tempts us to go against God's word, God's plans, God's best for our lives. He places the question in our minds of whether or not we can really trust God. He gets us to believe that we must "look out for number one" because no one else will. He doesn't care whether or not he gets the credit from us. His desire isn't to build his own kingdom as much as it is to destroy and steal from God's. He'll let you believe, as Haman did, that there wasn't more to what was happening than what human eyes could see. And, just as Haman deceived the king by making him believe that he was just looking out for his friend, the king, (when in reality, it wasn't about the king at all), Satan plants the idea in our minds that he is for us, that doing things our way (which is really his way) will bring us true satisfaction and fulfillment.

So, we see that the king trusted Haman so much, that he put the entire situation in his hands and allowed Haman to seek out whatever solution he wanted to design to take care of this "problem" of rebellious Israelites. The plan is laid out in verse 13. This verse parallels another verse we have all heard or read before: John 10:10 We all have an enemy and he is out to kill, steal, destroy—he doesn't play fair, he plays to win at all costs. He is never in any way sympathetic to our pain; he thrives on it and only wants more.

We'll go further into this in a later chapter. For now, ponder these questions and answer them honestly. Remember, God already knows the truth about where we are spiritually, and He loves us and accepts us right where we are. We can't go on to maturity without being honest about where we are today.

Prayer: "Heavenly Father, thank You for the truth You are teaching me; truth that reveals that You are truly in charge; that You don't change from one year or one generation to the next; truth that I can trust You completely. Thank You for being the Protector of my life; thank You that I don't have to fear the opposition, but rather in those times, I am being given an opportunity to draw closer to You."

Going Deeper to Understand My Purpose

1. Will you choose to allow God to have His will and way in your life to the point that you submit to the suffering that will result?

2. OR, will you choose to try to take control of the wheel and do things your way, realizing TODAY, if never before, that you will suffer even more going that route?

3. Being completely honest with God and yourself, on a scale of 1-10 where 1 is lowest and 10 is highest, where would you rank yourself in the area of your personal level of trust in God? Is your trust level growing, or was there a time when you felt you could trust God more than you do right now? Why?

4. What are the idols God is revealing are in your life? Are you willing to turn to God from those idols?

5. Describe as much as you know about your "identity in Christ"? What does that phrase mean to you personally? How would you describe your identity in Christ?

6. Where do you sense opposition in your life today? How have you been handling it thus far? Are there any changes you'll make as a result of the truths you're learning?

Just a note—none of the questions asked are meant to cause shame or embarrassment or even guilt. I journal a lot myself, and I love to look back and see where the Lord has brought me from and see the growth in my life. Remember, even if your trust level is in the negative right now, God's grace is still for you. You are loved and accepted right where you are. None of us is where we need to be yet, but thankfully, we have the Holy Spirit leading us on to greater depth of relationship and maturity. Being honest with where you are is the first step of growing to where God wants you to be.

CHAPTER 6

"I have some good news, and I have some bad news." (Part 1)

❧

Esther 3:13

"Letters were sent by couriers to each of the royal provinces [telling the officials] to destroy, kill, and annihilate all the Jewish people—young and old, women and children—and plunder their possessions on a single day, the thirteenth day of Adar, the twelfth month."

(Holman Christian Standard Bible; chosen for wording of this verse)

I pray the Lord is showing you much as you study the life of Esther. I so want this to be meaningful and in no way a waste of your time or energy. I have confidence that the Lord is teaching you through this study because He always honors His Word. For this chapter, I want to focus on one verse in particular from Esther along with one verse from John because these verses and the truths they hold have really impacted my own life as well as the lives of many others. Take a look and see what Jesus said in John 10:10:

> *"The thief comes <u>only</u> in order to steal and kill and destroy. I came that they may have and enjoy life, and have it in abundance (to the full, till it overflows)."*
> *(Amplified Bible, emphasis mine)*

You know the saying that goes, "Do you want the good news first, or the bad news?" Well, I usually choose the bad news in order to get that out of the way so that I can move on to the good news—I like something good to look forward to! So, we're going to start with the bad news in this chapter, so that we can end with some wonderfully GOOD news in the next chapter. Ready?

John 10:10a says, "The thief (Satan) does not come except to steal, to kill and to destroy."(NKJV) That is the reality of the enemy we all have; he doesn't even bother with us *except* to steal, kill and destroy. He is not an enemy that shows any compassion, nor does he relent from hurting us. His *only* motive is our destruction. He absolutely, passionately hates God and all that God loves. In Esther 3:13, we read a verse that tells us a little more how unfair and full of hate this enemy is. It says that the plan of attack was *"to destroy, to kill and to annihilate ALL of the Jewish people—young and old, women and children—and plunder their possessions..."* WOW! We have already read that in Haman's hatred for Mordecai, he became an enemy of the Jews, set himself up as his own god, and was in reality an instrument in Satan's hands. Haman's plan was Satan's plan. The Messiah was promised to the world through the Jewish people, so Satan did everything he could think of doing in order to destroy these people before God could fulfill His promise.

I want to go a little further with this in this chapter because *every one of us has been impacted by the enemy's plans.* He is out to steal, kill and destroy, and he doesn't wait until we are spiritually mature or full of God's Word before he begins his attacks. He doesn't even wait until we're saved! Did you see the verse in Esther? Even the children were to be destroyed. I have a four-year old son whom I am absolutely wildly in love with. I tell my husband that I had no idea I could love two men at the same time like this! He is absolutely precious to my entire family. Can you imagine me sending that innocent little guy to fight in the war in Iraq? He would be totally unprepared for a battle of that magnitude. He would be easy prey, wouldn't he? Picture with me a little one trying to handle a battle like that, trying desperately to figure out the rules, how to survive, how to use the weapons of warfare. Now, imagine an enemy *willing* to go to battle against that young, innocent child. This is an enemy of incredible wickedness. One who would prey on young, weak, immature, ill-equipped children is an enemy that is brutal and evil. THAT is the kind of enemy we all face. He isn't interested in waiting until we have grown physically, mentally, or spiritually. He is after the ones God loves and he attacks as early as he possibly can. Most of the deepest wounds we face are the ones that were inflicted upon us as children. Even though we can look with adult eyes and minds and see how we may have misunderstood, misconceived or actually been horribly victimized, as children we are left to make sense of the experiences with our very limited understanding. Just as Satan lied to Eve so long ago in the Garden of Eden, and twisted the words of God to confuse her and deceive her, he does so to us as well. He wants us to believe that God isn't as good as He says He is and that He is holding out on us. And in his plans to destroy us he doesn't wait until we're all grown up, spiritually or physically, before he begins his assault on us. His plans of attack are brutal and well-thought-out. God has taken me through some very painful experiences which are helping me to know His heart and who He truly is better than I could have without the pain. I can't tell you in one chapter (or even one book for that matter) how many lies I have believed as a child of God. I wouldn't have time to explain all of my own misunderstandings and misconceptions of my heavenly Daddy based on the experiences of my life beginning very early in my childhood. I heard someone once say that Satan isn't so interested in getting us to behave wrong as much as he is interested in getting us to *believe* wrong. If he can convince us to believe lies, about God, about ourselves and about life in general, then he has won a very significant battle.

We all have an enemy, and he is out to steal, to kill and to destroy. He begins the assault from conception as is obvious by the number of abortions committed worldwide in any given day. He continues his assault until we who are believers in Christ reach the other side. He isn't interested in you *except* to annihilate you. He will use any instrument available to bring his assault on your life. There is a saying that goes "Hurt people hurt people." As my husband and I work with hurting people from all walks of life, from men and women who struggle with life dominating addictions to people who have been wounded in full-time ministry, we find a very common denominator among them all—shame.

"Shame is the inner sense of being completely diminished or insufficient as a person. Self-judging self. A moment of shame may be humiliation so painful or an indignity so profound that one feels one has been robbed of his dignity or exposed as basically inadequate, bad, or worthy of rejection. A pervasive sense of shame is the on-going premise that one is fundamentally bad, inadequate, defective, unworthy, or not fully valued as a human being." (Fossum. Mason. (1986). Facing Shame Families in Recovery. W.W. Norton & Company, Inc. New York, NY Pg. 5) For so many, this sense of shame is inflicted in childhood. It could come from

overt abusiveness inflicted upon that child; it can happen through situations that were never meant to cause shame, but happened as accidental or without even realizing it; it can also come from the perceptions that can mislead a child to believe wrongly about him/herself. When I first started doing my studies in our church's lay counselor training class, I was extremely discouraged about the fact that I had children. I read book after book which explained the "ideal" way to parent children, and I knew I had failed time after time. I felt helpless and hopeless of ever being able to make up for my own shortcomings as a parent as I reflected and realized how I had been negatively impacted by my own parents' influences and choices. What a burden to try to be perfect so our children will grow up to be healthy adults who contribute positively to the world. Then, as I prayed so passionately for God to help me understand all of this, to understand why He would even allow imperfect people to become parents in the first place, He spoke so gently to my spirit when He said, "Shelley, even if I made you a perfect parent, it still wouldn't guarantee that your children will 'turn out' the way you believe they should. Even if you were absolutely perfect, they would still have an enemy who is out to steal, to kill and to destroy. He will do what he can to distort the good you do and overemphasize the wrong you do in order to annihilate them. THAT is why YOU need ME and THEY need ME. THAT is why I sent my Son." So parents, take heart. We all desperately need a Savior! I need one, my parents need one, my children need one; and so do you.

There is another saying I've heard that goes perfectly with what we're studying today: "Satan has many tools, but a lie is the handle that fits them all." (*Source unknown*) He will do whatever he can do to convince you that God isn't really as good as He says He is; that God cannot be trusted; that you aren't one of the ones God really loves; and he'll point to all the disappointing circumstantial evidence of your life experiences to do just that. If he can keep us from trusting God, he doesn't have to worry about our living lives of eternal and victorious impact. If we become convinced that God cannot be trusted, we'll take the matter of our lives into our own hands and live out of fear, not love. We'll be controlling, not giving of ourselves. We'll find ourselves in unhealthy relationships time and again, rather than true, authentic relationships where we know and are truly known. Satan hates you and wants to destroy you in any way he possibly can. If he can keep you from trusting God for salvation...wow, what a devastating thing. If he can't, he will continue lying to you once you become a child of God in order to keep you from living the abundant life promised to each of us by God Himself.

Not all people are impacted by shame to the same degree. Each person has unique and individual experiences because we are each unique and individual beings. Some of us are impacted greatly by shame and it filters everything in our lives in a negative, and possibly even "toxic", way. Some of us are less impacted and even had wonderful childhood relationships and experiences, with a pretty blessed life even now, which can lead us to believe we have *never* been impacted by shame. The reality is that being in a sin-cursed world is enough to cause each and every one of us to be affected in one way or another by this ugly reality. Even Adam and Eve who had never experienced verbal, physical, or sexual abuse felt shame simply because of their interrupted relationship with God through their sinful choice to disobey the one and only "do not" God gave to them. Before God ever confronted either of them about what they had done, they felt the desire to hide who they were and hide from God because of the shame they felt. For me, I didn't even realize the shame in my life until God revealed it to me by showing me all the negative ways I interpreted events in my life. In fact, He still has to remind me from time to time when I fall back into those old patterns of thinking.

Shame--it's such an ugly thing, and the enemy uses it in such incredibly wounding ways whenever and wherever he can. You and I, my friend, have an enemy whose only pleasure is destroying us to hurt God.

That is the bad news.

Prayer: If you have children in your life, pray for them today that God would protect them from the lies of the enemy that they may see God for who He is. Pray that the cycle of deceit would not be passed on to them. Pray for the generation coming behind you. Pray for yourself as well—ask the Lord to reveal the lies you've believed that have caused you to see God differently than how He describes Himself in His Word.

Going Deeper to Understand My Purpose:

The Bad News:

1. How have you been affected by the "bad news" — by the plots and schemes of the enemy? Where can you see that he has set out to kill, to steal, and to destroy?

2. What lies have you believed? If you can't think of anything, ask God to search your heart and reveal to you where you may be believing lies about Him and even lies about yourself.

3. I Peter 5:8 –*"Be well balanced (temperate, sober of mind), be vigilant and cautious at all times; for that enemy of yours, the devil, roams around like a lion roaring [[[]a[]]in fierce hunger], seeking someone to seize upon and devour." (AMP.)*

A. Where do you sense the enemy scheming in your life even today?

B. Where do you see a need for balance in your life so that you can stand firm against the enemy's lies and attacks?

C. Realizing the devil is seeking someone out to seize upon and devour, what do you believe are your greatest weapons against defeat?

D. How are you implementing those weapons in your daily life?

Note: Some of us have been so impacted by the lies and abuses of the enemy and even those around us that we might need the help of a trained Christian counselor to help us sort through the painful things we are experiencing. We're going to discuss the good news in the next chapter, but don't wait to get help if you need it. Take advantage of what is available to you, and if the help of a counselor would benefit you, don't waste that opportunity. The abundant life is yours for the claiming!

CHAPTER 7

"I have some good news, and I have some bad news." (Part 2)

❧

Esther 3:13

"Letters were sent by couriers to each of the royal provinces [telling the officials] to destroy, kill, and annihilate all the Jewish people—young and old, women and children—and plunder their possessions on a single day, the thirteenth day of Adar, the twelfth month."

(Holman Christian Standard Bible; chosen for wording of this verse)

I couldn't wait to get to this chapter! I hate ending on a bad note, so this chapter will be full of *great* news. I am *absolutely thrilled* to be able to tell you that although in reality there IS bad news for all of us to accept, there is also some very, very good news!! John 10:10b says that although there is a ruthless, heartless, cruel enemy ready to take us down, Jesus, our Savior, came to earth for a purpose as well, and in His own words, He said of Himself, "...I have come that they may have life and have it more abundantly." Or, as the Message translation says, "A thief is only there to steal and kill and destroy. *I came so they can have real and eternal life, more and better life than they ever dreamed of.*" (Emphasis mine) *This* is the good news of the Gospel of Christ! Most of us have only accepted half of the gospel message which is that Jesus died for us so that we could one day live with Him in heaven and miss hell. But there is so much more! He didn't just die so that when we die we wouldn't go to hell (even though that truly IS wonderful news and is grace in and of itself!); He also died so we could live, really live, here, while we're still on earth, still on this side of eternity. Jesus tells us we *do* have an enemy, we *do* have someone who is out to get us, but it's not God! Many of us come to the conclusion (even if we won't admit it to ourselves) that God isn't *really* all that good. Larry Crabb said in his book, The Safest Place on Earth, "We simply do not believe in a God who is so intrinsically good that His desire to be fully Himself is equivalent to His desire to be very good to us." And how do we arrive at that conclusion? Through our experiences in life. Russell Willingham, in his book, Relational Masks, said that our "concept of God is based on both Scripture and our pain." Satan wants us to believe that the good, abundant life is for *others* (if for anyone) but never for "me". We find ourselves comparing our own situations and experiences with that of others and we come to believe that God's good promises don't seem to be for us. Sure, the Word of God tells me those promises and I *theologically* agree with those promises, but when it comes down to how I live my life on a daily basis, my mind and my heart don't meet up with one another.

If you're anything like me, you may have tried to gain God's favor and approval with your service to Him, only finding yourself burned out and exhausted, never feeling that He is satisfied with you. We have many, many well intentioned people in our churches serving their hearts out and wondering why others aren't doing it. I believe that it's because our beliefs are confused. Some people understand grace to mean they have no responsibilities now, that they're free from rules, so now they don't have to do anything. They are partly right. Others believe that if a person is truly grateful for God's gift of salvation then they will spend all of their lives doing whatever they can do to pay God back, or show their gratitude to Him, by serving Him. After all He has done for us, He deserves this right? They, too, are partly right. There is a divine balance between grace and truth. Jesus was the only One able to live this out perfectly, which qualified *Him*, and *Him alone*, to be our standard in this all-important aspect to the victorious Christian life.

I spent most of my Christian life (and I was saved when I was only five years old) trying to be a good girl for God. I wanted desperately to be one of the ones He would use in big ways—or *any* significant way for that matter. I tried so hard following the "formula" for Christian living, and never seemed to measure up. I was extremely hard on myself and very judgmental of those who wouldn't toe the line, and even though I knew that I couldn't do it either, "at least I was trying", I would think to myself. Grace to me meant that I didn't have to go to hell, but would go to heaven one day. I wonder as I write this how many people can relate to this belief. Any little mistake I would make, I felt like, put me back to the starting line of this Christian race, and that I had to make it up to God for what I had done. There was no rest. There was little relationship with God. It was all about me trying to earn God's favor *this* side of salvation. I could go on and on about how Scripture speaks to this. Paul wrote his letter to the Galatians because they were caught up in this as well. The Book of Romans speaks so clearly about the grace of God that not only saves us but keeps us in God's favor here on earth. His *favor*...think of what that means to be in God's favor. Webster's dictionary defines it this way: *"friendly regard shown toward another especially by a superior; approving consideration or attention; gracious kindness"*. God, our divine Superior, has shown us friendly regard, approving consideration and attention, and gracious kindness. Wow! How many of us truly believe that God's favor is upon us? Right where we are, with all that we have done, with all that has been done TO us, with all the sin surrounding us—*There is no other word for grace than Amazing!* When we capture this as <u>truth for us,</u> there is no other response than worship. Worship leads us into God's presence and in God's presence we enjoy fellowship and relationship with Him, and once we have tasted and seen that the Lord is indeed very good, a desire is born within us to allow Him to have His way in our lives, understanding that His plans for us are the best, most-fulfilling, satisfying plans imaginable. There simply are no greater plans for us than God's plans.

In Esther's life, she *had* to be born in the culture and time of history in which she was born; she *had* to be orphaned; she *had* to be placed in Mordecai's home; and she *had* to be taken from that home and placed in the harem of the king. All of these things *had* to happen. In God's divine wisdom, He knows the plans that He has for us, and as I quoted the song in an earlier chapter, He also knows the means of bringing those plans together. Everything Esther went through and experienced, good and bad, prepared her for what God was preparing *for* her.

In my life, I *had* to be born into an imperfect family (weren't we all?); I *had* to experience the pain of sexual abuse; I *had* to experience the devastation of divorce—both my parents and my own; I *had* to experience the pain of loss through multiple miscarriages. I've heard people say that they believe God will use me more because of these ugly experiences, but I think it's more than that. I believe God can use any of us more when we realize how broken we are apart from Him, how needy we are of Him. And, in His abundant grace and goodness, He will do exactly what is necessary, and allow whatever is necessary to bring us to that place. God has been and still is in the process of *preparing me* for what He has prepared *for* me. This truth is exciting to me! Most of us can handle anything if we know it is worth it. And, to me, knowing God to the extent that I do *today* makes all of the pain to get me here worth it.

So, if Jesus came to give us life, better life than we ever dreamed of, what exactly does that kind of life look like? I believe the abundant life is this:

It's a life lived out of God's grace and God's truth based on the foundation of knowing God intimately through His Word.

Grace says that because of God's love and Christ's sacrifice, we get to be fully acceptable to God right now. Truth says that although we're fully accepted right now, there is quite a bit of maturing yet to do. Grace allows me to enjoy intimacy with God regardless of my level of maturity. Truth allows me to see where I am today and gives me guidelines for growth in my relationship with God. Grace says I don't have to do anything I don't want to do and God will still love and accept me. Truth tells me that if I choose to be lazy in this life, I will have nothing to offer Jesus when I get home except regrets, and many regrets at that. The truth is, if I truly understand God's grace, the way scripture reveals it, it won't hinder my service or commitment to the Lord; it will only enhance it and empower me *to walk* in that tightrope balance of grace and truth as I yield my will to God's will. I often pray, "Lord, may the influence of my flesh decrease and may the influence of the Spirit of God in me increase." If you're a child of the Most High God, then you have the Spirit of the living God residing in you, empowering you to live, and move, and be. Many people in the Church are afraid of teaching grace for the fear that people will misinterpret the teaching to mean they are free to do whatever they want, and therefore, no one will do anything and so nothing will get done. I often find that the Church unintentionally uses guilt and pressure to cajole and "motivate" people into serving. This often seemingly works when people jump up and get busy serving, for a time, but if people are serving only out of a sense of relieving their guilt, out of a sense of duty and pressure, these same people who start out strong will sooner or later come to a crossroads of the Christian life. On one path, they can continue serving and submitting out of a sense of duty, pride, guilt, ambivalence, etc. These people might even be very sincere in their desire to please God, their friends, their church leaders, and their own consciences. On the other path, they will be able to say "no" to good things, even when people get upset and think badly of them, because they'll be so freed up to allow the Christ-life to flow through them. These people, on the second path, will be the ones who continue, with joy and enthusiasm, to serve the Lord wholeheartedly because they will be living with the truth and grace that says they are already fully accept-able and pleasing to God because of Jesus Christ. These are the people who can handle conviction of sin, need for growth and change, and even disapproval of others because they live with the confidence that the One who knows them best, accepts and delights in them the most. When conviction comes, it does not bring condemnation. When the disapproval of others comes, and it will, they can handle this with grace and tact, knowing that it will be impossible to please everyone all the time, and that is okay!

The Apostle Paul had to deal with this issue and taught the grace of God boldly. (See Romans 6-8 for just one of many examples.) I've learned that people can take anything Scripture teaches and distort it to match their preferences, but when people allow the truth to penetrate their hearts, God changes lives in a dramatic way. (See Romans 12:1-2.) So, the choice becomes ours to make. Many people use their interpretation of grace to live in sinfulness. Others use their interpretation of truth to hold themselves or others in bondage and to control behavior. Neither is representing the heart of our Father because neither is completely true to His own words. In order to live the abundant life Jesus offers, we must choose to allow Him to live His life through us in balance of grace *and* truth.

My husband recently introduced me to a devotional book called <u>The Green Letters</u> written by Miles J. Stanford. In one chapter, entitled "Help", the author says, *"For most of us, it is time to stop asking God for help. He didn't help us to be saved, and He doesn't intend to help us live the Christian life. Immaturity considers the Lord Jesus a Helper. Maturity knows Him to be Life itself."* This I had to read, and reread to get the full impact of what he was saying. I myself often pray for God's help to live in grace and truth, to help me be strong, to help me do the right thing, to strengthen me so that I can be victorious. There are far too many Christians, including myself, still asking for help to do what God has already done *in* them, and for help to live the life Jesus will live *through* them, if they'll just relinquish the control of their entire beings to Him, and allow Him to live that balance of grace and truth *through* them.

A balance of grace and truth in my life equips me to live "above my circumstances", meaning that I can be joyful in any and every circumstance no matter how much money I make, or don't make; where I live; what I drive (or don't drive); my marital status; health; job; calling; etc. Many of us believe that the abundant life is a life of comfort, ease, and living on the path of least resistance. No wonder we often throw in the towel when a trial, a temptation, or a time of testing comes our way! Our definition of "abundant living" isn't based on the Bible.

The abundant life has to do with knowing God intimately. When we make the decision to accept God's gift of salvation through Jesus Christ, and Him alone, we enter into a personal relationship with God Almighty. At the point of salvation, we are given everything we need pertaining to life and godliness. (II Peter 1:3) When we get to know God intimately, (which is a process that comes over time just like any other relationship), we begin to trust Him in a way most Christians never realize in their entire lives. When we make the commitment to get to know God, He transforms our thinking which transforms our feelings and changes our behavior patterns. (Romans 12:1-2) He works on us from the inside out. Most people want outside change to come first so that we can feel better about ourselves on the inside (our thoughts and emotions) and feel more acceptable to others. God is all-knowing and all-wise and knows that working on us from the inside (who we really are) will yield fruit on the outside. We often think if things on the outside could be different, (i.e. our circumstances, finances, relationships, etc.), then we could enjoy the abundant life and hence feel good inside. Sometimes we think if we can just master our behaviors, then the blessings of God will fall on us. But God knows the truly abundant life is the life that is lived from the inside out, rather than the other way around. He knows that "behavior management" doesn't change anyone. That is why He goes straight to our hearts.

I believe this is why the Apostle Paul was able to boast about his God when he told of learning contentment in any and every situation. He had gotten to know God intimately and thus realized that whether he was sitting in a palace with power or in a prison as a pauper, he could enjoy God and live abundantly. Don't you want to be there, too? I know I do! And I'm thankful to know that God won't give up on the process of maturing me to that point if I'll continue to be pliable and teachable in the process.

John 8:31-32 says, "If you abide in My word you are My disciples indeed. *Then* you will know the truth and the truth will make you free." (NKJV; Emphasis mine.) Make the conscience choice to go to God's Word in order to get to know the TRUTH. You *cannot* walk in freedom apart from knowing the truth. No longer simply "believing", but knowing. Sure, you can behave right for a while without knowing the truth, and you might even think that means you're free, but if you're not living based on truth, you're still in shackles to the wrong beliefs you have including the belief that God is *only,* or at the very least, *primarily* concerned with how you behave.

How will you know when someone, including this teacher, is telling you the truth if you don't go to the source of truth for yourself? Many believers are living in bondage to sin, to their circumstances, and even to the enemy because they haven't invested in learning truth. They go from one conference to another trying to feast on what others have learned, but never learn how to feed themselves. It's tragic how many people are falling for whatever enthusiastic teacher professes as truth. Get into the manual of truth for yourself and let God teach you who He is, who you are in Christ, and what your purpose is for this generation. We've all heard the saying by now, I'm sure: "Only one life, 'twill soon be past. Only what's done for Christ will last!" Do you want your life to count? Do you want to enjoy the abundant life God offers to each and every believer? Then don't give up my friend. Keep on pressing into the Word of God and allow Him to transform your mind, refresh your emotions, and change your behavior to the glory of God. Be the one who determines from here on out, "I will live my life on purpose!"

> *Prayer:"Lord Jesus, Thank you for your grace that makes me fully pleasing and fully acceptable to you. Thank you for truth that takes me on to maturity. Help me to live in the balance. Thank you for conquering the power of sin and taking down the enemy who so desires to have me. Help me to walk in grace and truth, as I get to know You more intimately, which will lead me to victory."*

Going Deeper to Understand My Purpose:

The Good News

1. Many people see the "abundant life" as a problem-free, financially well-to-do kind of life. After reading today's lesson, what do you make of all of this?

2. Before this lesson, had someone asked you, how would you have defined "the abundant life" Jesus promised?

3. Are you, today, living the "abundant life"? How do you know? Give examples.

4. How have you been living thus far in the matter of grace and truth?

5. Do you see yourself living in consistent balance? If not, do you see yourself more on the grace side or on the truth side?

6. What is God showing you about yourself and how to live in greater balance of both grace and truth?

7. In light of John 8:31-32, what can you do to be more intentional in getting to know God better for yourself?

CHAPTER 8

"For Such a Time as This"

Esther 3:14-4:14

"14 A copy of the writing was to be published and giv–
en out as a decree in every province to all the peoples
to be ready for that day. 15The special messengers
went out in haste by order of the king, and the decree
was given out in Shushan, the capital. And the king
and Haman sat down to drink, but the city of Shushan
was perplexed [at the strange and alarming decree].

Esther 4

1NOW WHEN Mordecai learned all that was done,
[he] rent his clothes and put on sackcloth with ashes and
went out into the midst of the city and cried with a loud
and bitter cry. 2He came and stood before the king's
gate, for no one might enter the king's gate clothed
with sackcloth. 3And in every province, wherever the
king's commandment and his decree came, there was
great mourning among the Jews, with fasting, weeping,
and wailing, and many lay in sackcloth and ashes.
4When Esther's maids and her attendants came and

told it to her, the queen was exceedingly grieved and distressed. She sent garments to clothe Mordecai, with orders to take his sackcloth from off him, but he would not receive them. 5Then Esther called for Hathach, one of the king's attendants whom he had appointed to attend her, and ordered him to go to Mordecai to learn what this was and why it was. 6So Hathach went out to Mordecai in the open square of the city, which was in front of the king's gate. 7And Mordecai told him of all that had happened to him, and the exact sum of money that Haman had promised to pay to the king's treasuries for the Jews to be destroyed. 8[Mordecai] also gave him a copy of the decree to destroy them, that was given out in Shushan, that he might show it to Esther, explain it to her, and charge her to go to the king, make supplication to him, and plead with him for the lives of her people. 9And Hathach came and told Esther the words of Mordecai. 10Then Esther spoke to Hathach and gave him a message for Mordecai, saying, 11All the king's servants and the people of the king's provinces know that any person, be it man or woman, who shall go into the inner court to the king without being called shall be put to death; there is but one law for him, except [him] to whom the king shall hold out the golden scepter, that he may live. But I have not been called to come to the king for these thirty days. 12And they told Mordecai what Esther said. 13Then Mordecai told them to return this answer to Esther, Do not flatter yourself that you shall escape in the king's palace any more than all the other Jews. 14For if you keep silent at this time, relief and deliverance shall arise for the Jews from elsewhere, but you and your father's house will perish. And who knows but that you have come to the kingdom for such a time as this and for this very occasion?" (Amplified Bible)

The Casual Response of those in Authority

Did you see that? Right after this horrible decree goes out to all the people so that they know what is planned, the king and Haman "sat down to drink". This is unbelievable! Total annihilation is planned for an entire people group, and the ones planning it just casually sit and enjoy a drink together! It seems unthinkable to me, but some commentators have suggested that Persian kings *customarily* drank and were often *inebriated* (drunk!) while making weighty decisions. (Think back to his condition when he made the decision about Vashti.) King Solomon spoke of the importance of a king being sober-minded as a ruler, which set Godly kings apart from the normal customs of pagan rulers. It appears that since this king bought the deceit of Haman, he casually went about business as usual giving little or no thought to what he had allowed. He had no idea he had just signed his beloved wife's death certificate in allowing Haman to execute his plot. But, perhaps there is more history to this than we might realize if we just look at *this* story, found in the book of Esther, without knowing the rest of the story. Let's take a look at that now.

When we read the book of Ezra, we find out that King Ahasuerus had possibly already formed a negative opinion of the Israelites. In his first year as king, some men who couldn't dissuade the Israelites from rebuilding their temple wrote to King Ahasuerus to get him to stop them. Read Ezra 4:6 "And in the reign of Ahasuerus [or Xerxes], in the beginning of his reign, [the Samaritans] wrote to him an accusation against the [returned] inhabitants of Judah and Jerusalem." (Amplified Bible) Later on that same group tried to appeal to his son, Artaxerxes. Apparently, King Ahasuerus had already dealt with some matters between Jews and non-Jews and had, since early on in his reign, believed them to be untrustworthy and therefore deserving of Haman's plans for their annihilation. Additionally, King Ahasuerus was now not doing as well financially due to his unsuccessful attempt at overtaking Greece and it is suggested by some that this made Haman's plan seem even more attractive to the king.

And as far as Haman is concerned, he apparently thought that taking matters into his own hands would bring him the satisfaction we often think we'll get if we avenge ourselves. He was so full of rage toward Mordecai and believed he could make himself feel better by destroying Mordecai and everything he stood for. Haman wasn't a follower of Jehovah. He, like King Ahasuerus, was a lost man behaving like a lost man.

For the believer, here is at least one area of application for us today. God's word tells us "vengeance is Mine, says the Lord, I will repay." (Deut. 32:35; Rom. 12:19; Heb. 10:30) As I look at the examples set in this story, I need to realize that it is not up to me to avenge myself by trying to pay people back for what they have done to me. We all deal with difficult people. Not one of us will go through life and never have an enemy. It is often, at least for me, so tempting to try to make things even or prove, somehow, that the other person is wrong so that I can feel validated. Here are some verses I go to in order to remember what God has to say to me about this very subject:

Romans 12:17 says, "Do not repay anyone evil for evil. Be careful to do what is right in the eyes of everybody."

1 Peter 3:9 "Do not repay evil with evil or insult with insult, but with blessing, because to this you were called so that you may inherit a blessing."
Proverbs 20:22 "Do not say, I will repay evil; wait [expectantly] for the Lord, and He will rescue you." (Amplified Bible)

Haman had no idea that the pit he was digging for others would be the very one he himself would fall into. Proverbs 26:27 says, "If you set a trap for others, you will get caught in it yourself. If you roll a boulder down on others, it will roll back and crush you." (The Message)

What I have seen in my own life has shown me that God really is true to His word. I have had difficult relationship issues and have often wanted to set that other person straight, to defend myself, and sometimes even to get back at him/her for what was done to me. But there is a really fine line between confrontation for *reconciliation* and confrontation for *revenge*. We must allow the Holy Spirit to test our hearts to find our true motive for confronting. What I have been told in several instances is to be still and wait, to show kindness when given opportunity for it, and to hold my tongue, carefully weighing what I will and will not say. I can say that on more than one occasion, God did His work better without my interference and even brought healing to relationships because I was able not to rush to action, but rather allow Him to work in the other person's heart and life as He was also working in mine. Don't seek revenge, my friend. Let God **be** God.

The Chaotic Response of the People

In this part of the story, we not only see the *casual response* of those in authority, we also see the understandable *chaotic response* of the Jewish people. *(Ch. 4:1-7)* Naturally, everyone panicked. Where they had just been going about "business as usual", minding their own business, living their lives; now, suddenly, in one moment's time, (reading the decree), all of life changed *instantly*. Just as the people of Israel, God's people had no idea that life could change so dramatically and in such a devastating way, we, too, have no guarantee that calamity won't come upon us in a moment. How many of us have already experienced this? Who can forget September 11,

2001? I, like you, remember exactly where I was and what I was doing when I heard what was happening. As I write this, our nation is in mourning after a gunman chose to take the lives of 32 people, including his own, at Virginia Tech on April 16, 2007—the deadliest crime of this kind in the history of the U.S. I can imagine you have personal experiences of when life changed forever for you in an instant. Life can change in the smallest moment for good and for bad. *In those moments what we choose to do matters significantly.* What makes the biggest difference, I believe, is how we have been living and relating to God up to that point. Do we have a strong foundation built upon solid rock that will withstand the fiercest winds and driving rains of the most powerful and difficult storms in our lives? Proverbs 24:10 in the NIV says, "If you falter in times of trouble, how small is your strength." Look at what the Message says in that same verse: "If you fall to pieces in a crisis, there wasn't much to you in the first place." Wow! When I see someone go through a crisis of some kind, and all of a sudden you don't see that person in church (I don't mean for a season, I mean for a long period of time), and he/she is no longer walking with God, or in a season of temptation or trial of testing, they give in and make an obviously sinful choice, it begs the question--What kind of foundation had they been building up to this point? I don't mean this to be harsh or judgmental; I just say it as a warning and as an encouragement to us all. When someone has something wonderful happen to them suddenly, there is that same challenge of remaining faithful and remembering that we are all dependent on God even in the most affluent, healthy, blessed, and enjoyable days of our lives. Build the foundation because you WILL need it sooner or later.

Fortunately for the Jewish people living in Susa, Mordecai and Esther had invested in their relationship with God and in one another. Because of this, there was a strong foundation in place so that they didn't fall apart when this awful day came. And, as we'll see later, when God allowed Esther and Mordecai to experience His abundant blessings, the foundation kept their spiritual house in place then as well.

The Courageous Response of God's Chosen

Our heroes in this story respond in a way that is an example for all of us. Not only did we see the *casual response* of the perpetrators, the *chaotic response* of the victims, but now we see **the *courageous response* of God's chosen.** Mordecai and Esther give us an incredible example of how to respond when calamity comes our way. In addition to the firm foundation that was in place, we also see something else.

❖ The importance of **COMPLETE HONESTY**

In Mordecai's life we can see that because he had remained faithful to the Lord up to this point, he was able to stand firm in this crucial moment of his life. He felt the emotions and expressed them honestly. He didn't bottle up his emotions in an attempt to show bravery, he courageously expressed his emotions openly.

Think about it for a moment; try to place yourself in Mordecai's situation. You've shown allegiance, wholeheartedly, to the One True God. You meant it when you sang, "Though none go with me, I still will follow." When your orphaned relative needed a place to live, you offered your home and became a parent to her. When she was taken to a pagan king's harem, you kept in contact with her through others to maintain that bond and close relationship. When you heard there was a threat against that king, you spoke up and prevented an assassination, getting nothing in return, not even a "thank you for saving my life" note in the mail. When a wicked enemy of your God, and your people, required your homage, you refused to bow and stood up for the One and only God, knowing it could cost you your life but never anticipating that this could cost anyone else his life, much less the lives of ALL of your people as well. Remember Esther 3:13? No one, not even the smallest child, would be spared. Mordecai's grief and fear were very, very real. If you can identify with any of these questions of his, then it means you've been to that dark night of the soul yourself. You've experienced the questions, even if you refused to ask them: "Why would God allow this?" "Why is God doing this to me?" "What have I done or not done that would justify this?" "What can I do to get out of this; it's too much!" If you can't, then hold on, and keep your focus on God while being a faithful student of His Word. Your time will come. Because of His love and grace and mercy, He will take us through the fires of testing in order to burn off everything that doesn't reflect His image. The tests don't come to see if we'll pass or fail. Our westernized minds often assume this is the case. The tests come to show us what is true about our spiritual condition. When a goldsmith tests gold, he places it in intense heat that the impurities, *which he expects to find*, will rise to the surface that he might remove them, purifying the gold. He doesn't put it in the fires of testing to see if it will pass or fail as gold, he knows that what he is testing is gold. *He tests it to purify it.* This is what God does in our lives as well. As the Master Goldsmith, He puts us through fiery tests to give us opportunities to allow Him to do a work of grace in our lives that will transform us and make us more like His dear Son. Understanding this more has helped me to expect and even rest in His love for me when the tests come.

Mordecai's hope, I believe, came from the fact that he knew the Lord had placed Esther in this place of prominence for a reason that was far bigger than simply allowing her to enjoy the comforts of the kingdom. Everything in her life and everything about her was for such a significant purpose. Realizing this truth even in the midst of unbearable pain, gave him the hope that if God's sovereignty placed her there, then

God's sovereignty would protect her there. With this reality in mind, he confronted Esther about a difficult choice she would have to make. This woman was not just a queen to him; this was his beloved Hadasseh. Going to her to tell her what she must do had to be very difficult. Don't forget, this is the man who paced back and forth daily just to hear some word of how she was doing. Those of us with children can understand that it is a greater challenge when we have to watch our children suffer than when we have to suffer ourselves. I am confident if Mordecai believed there was some other way to effectively handle this dilemma he would have gladly chosen it. If it meant his own death, I can only imagine his willingness to offer himself rather than his child.

In Esther's life, we can imagine that Mordecai's words were not easy ones to accept. But because of their relationship, and Esther's ability to trust Mordecai, she didn't just go about her own business and ignore what he had told her. She investigated matters for herself. She was a woman of intelligence and confidence, and I think it is safe to say that she could contribute much of that to how she had been raised by this godly man. At first, Esther responded out of fear; she told Mordecai why she believed she could not obey his command. Maybe she thought he would be able to come up with an alternative to her having to break the law by inviting herself into the king's presence. She told him it could cost her her very life if she went to the king uninvited. This wasn't news to Mordecai, though. He already knew the law well. Her fear was very valid. After all, she was married to the man who divorced Vashti and sent her away because she refused to come when summoned. The laws were on the books; going into the king's presence uninvited was a huge risk to say the least. But think about this—how many times do we respond like this with God's commands? Out of our fear of the unknown future, the fear of what we think is inevitable, we tell Him why we simply cannot do what He asks us to do. This can be seen in our response to what His word says in regard to witnessing to lost people, in regard to trusting Him with our money, our children, careers, ministries, and even our lives.

As we look at the lives of Esther and Mordecai, we see that they were completely honest. They were in authentic relationship with one another where they could speak freely and be heard freely. But we also see the other side which kept this emotional part in balance.

❖ The importance of **COMPLETE OBEDIENCE**

Mordecai told Esther: verse 13-14, "(I)f you remain completely silent at this time, relief and deliverance will arise for the Jews from another place, but you and your fathers house will perish…" *If I fail to accept God's call upon my life, He will use someone else who is willing, and then I miss out on the blessing and protection offered.* Victory belongs to God either way! Because of this, I can walk confidently in obedience to God knowing that my protection comes from Him. Facing an unknown future is not nearly as frightening because of His sovereignty. My life is in HIS hands!

Take the Gospels for a quick example. When you read these four accounts, you'll find different occasions when Jesus could have been afraid of danger, but kept on going about his business because He knew "His time had not yet come." This gives me a great deal of comfort in my own life. God has numbered my *days* (Psalm 139). Nothing, absolutely nothing and no one can do anything to me until my time comes, and when my times comes, it's simply the pathway to my eternal home. Jesus knew this, and He rested securely in the Father's plans for Him.

"Ask for the victory, I will come and bring it. *Don't look for the victory—look for Me,* and you will see the victory that I will bring with Me."

Come Away My Beloved, Frances J. Roberts, Barbour Publishing

Esther, once refusing out of fear, now says, "If I perish, I perish!" This statement came as a result of her request for Mordecai and others to fast for three days in order to gain God's direction in what should be done. Her faith was strong enough to say, 'if God so chooses to call me to this, and I die, then so be it—I'll obey regardless.' This takes extreme faith that only comes through consistent obedience; consistent obedience that perseveres over time through the small trials and the big ones. This kind of faith doesn't happen by itself, nor does it come to "any and all"; this kind of faith takes our active participation in our relationship with God. As we make a decided effort to participate with God in this sanctification process, we move forward to a maturing relationship that can stand the tests and trials when (not *if*, but *when*) they come. This kind of faith comes as a result of hearing the Word and then doing it consistently—acting upon what I have received as truth. In James 1 we read that God wants us to be "doers of the word and not hearers only." This world has plenty of hearers, but far too few doers.

There is a balance to living the abundant life we're promised. We must choose to be honest, authentic and real, not pretending to be someone we're not, or to be where we'd like to be spiritually or otherwise, but be absolutely real. We need to recognize that we are all dependent beings—dependent on the same God to meet our needs. We also must choose to obey whether we feel like it or not; that is faith. Obey, based on who God is, not on your own understanding of the situation you face.

Proverbs 3:5-6
"Lean on, trust in, and be confident in the Lord with all your heart and mind and do not rely on your own insight or understanding. In all your ways know, recognize, and acknowledge Him, and He will direct and make straight and plain your paths." (Amplified Bible)

Please understand this. It isn't that our emotions don't matter; they are gifts and not curses. They matter tremendously, but in the midst of our feelings, good or bad, when we choose to obey with our wills, God is blessed and our faith is strengthened. Our relationship with God grows deeper and stronger as a result.

Esther knew that apart from praying fervently, which in this case included fasting, she would not be able to make a certain decision about what to do. As we go about our lives, how seriously do we take prayer? How seriously do we take the discipline of fasting?

Here are some quotes on prayer to ponder:

"Prayer does not equip us for greater works—prayer is the greater work."
~Oswald Chambers

"We have not proven the sufficiency of God until we have asked of Him the impossible."
~Unknown

"The most fundamental need, duty, honor, and happiness of man is not petition, nor even contrition, nor again even thanksgiving—these three kinds of prayer which, indeed, must never disappear out of our spiritual lives—but adoration."
~Freidrich Von Hugel

"We must alter our lives in order to alter our hearts, for it is impossible to live one way and pray another."
~William Law

"Any concern too small to be turned into a prayer is too small to be made into a burden."
~Corrie ten Boom

"All I have seen teaches me to trust the Creator for what I have not seen."
~Ralph Waldo Emerson

"We are all faced with great opportunities brilliantly disguised as impossible situations."
~Truett Cathy

"We all come to prayer with a tangled mass of motives—altruistic and selfish, merciful and hateful, loving and bitter. Frankly, this side of eternity we will never unravel the good from the bad, the loving and the bitter. But what I have come to see is that God is big enough to receive us with all our mixture. We do not have to be bright, or pure, or filled with faith, or anything. That is what grace means, and not only are we saved by grace, we live by it as well. And we pray by it."
~Richard Foster

Prayer: "Dear Gracious, Sovereign Father, in my quest to become all You would have me to be, help me to keep my focus on You more than on the goal of what I'd like to become. Help me to trust You with my pain. Thank you for the healing that You've already brought, and for the healing that is on its way. May I be used by You to make an eternal impact on this generation as I simply trust and obey."

Going Deeper to understand my purpose:

Ask yourself these questions:

1. Do I see myself growing in the area of authenticity with God and others?

2. What is an indicator of this that I am aware of?

3. In what way(s) do I see God's purposes for pain in my own life? (Note: *Sometimes God lets us see at least part of the plan to give us comfort for those times when we can't.)*

4. Where do I sense God is increasing my maturity the most right now?

5. What area is the area of greatest struggle?

6. Who or What is the "Haman" in my life?

    A. Am I willing to trust God in obedience and release this to Him in order that He might handle this for me?

    B. What has God told me is my responsibility in this situation? Am I willing to trust and obey?

7. Take some time to look up some verses on prayer. Write them down and then make note of what they are saying specifically to you. For example: Proverbs 3:5-6 "Trust in the Lord with all your heart and lean not on your own understanding. In all your ways acknowledge Him and He will direct your paths." *This says that if I will do my part, God will do His. Because I can trust that He is faithful, I can be more confident as I choose not to trust my own understanding of a situation, but rather choose to listen to Him and then obey what He says. He will make the way smooth and clear and lead me on to where I am supposed to be. This frees me up to enjoy Him and allow Him to have His way in my life.*

As we go about our week, let's not forget to be real about who we are, what we're going through, and to balance that with obedience to God's Word, praying fervently for ourselves and others, and as we do, being faithful to share the Good News that only Jesus—the reason for every season—offers.

CHAPTER 9

Esther's Banquet

Esther 5:1-8

"1ON THE third day [of the fast] Esther put on her royal robes and stood in the royal or inner court of the king's palace opposite his [throne room]. The king was sitting on his throne, facing the main entrance of the palace. 2And when the king saw Esther the queen standing in the court, she obtained favor in his sight, and he held out to [her] the golden scepter that was in his hand. So Esther drew near and touched the tip of the scepter. 3Then the king said to her, What will you have, Queen Esther? What is your request? It shall be given you, even to the half of the kingdom. 4And Esther said, If it seems good to the king, let the king and Haman come this day to the dinner that I have prepared for the king. 5Then the king said, Cause Haman to come quickly, that what Esther has said may be done. 6So the king and Haman came to the dinner that Esther had prepared. 7And during the serving of wine, the king said to Esther, What is your petition? It shall be granted you. And what is your request? Even to the half of the kingdom, it shall be performed. 8Then Esther said, My petition and my request is: If I have found favor in the sight of the king and if it pleases the king to grant my petition and to perform my request, let the king and Haman come tomorrow to the dinner that I shall prepare for them; and I will do tomorrow as the king has said." (Amplified Bible)

"When you pass through the waters, I will be with you; and when you pass through the rivers, they will not sweep over you. When you walk through the fire, you will not be burned; the flames will not set you ablaze."

Isaiah 43:2 (NKJV, emphasis mine)

God sees and rewards our faithfulness to Him

In this chapter, we're going to consider what this must have been like for Esther, to have been through everything she had experienced, and now to be faced with the greatest challenge of her life. I believe she knew that the only way she would make it was to depend on her God. Like Mordecai, her faithfulness up to this point prepared her for this challenge.

Sometimes we see people who are being used mightily for God and we think that there is some magic formula for this kind of "success"; that, perhaps, if we could figure out the formula, then we too could be used of God in great ways. Well, it's not magic; it is something far more real than that. And, it is no formula either, but I'll let you in on what makes some people useable by God in big ways. Ready? It is *faithfulness*. That's it? Can't there be more to it? Well, yes and no. True faithfulness, not simple performance to gain something, but real faithfulness and trust in God yields to a life of obedience, dedication, service, etc. I love the words of this old hymn, "When we walk with the Lord, in the light of His Word, what a glory He sheds on our way. While we do His good will, He abides with us still, and for ALL who will trust and obey. Trust and obey for there's no other way to be happy in Jesus, but to trust and obey." Esther had been trusting and obeying for some time before this opportunity from God presented itself. Yes, this was a great challenge and took a huge leap of faith, but more than anything, this was an opportunity for Esther to get in on what God was going to do in the lives of the people of her generation. She got to get in on it!! I want that; I want to be so faithful and to trust in such a way, that God can present opportunity after opportunity for me to be used of Him to make eternal impact for good in my own generation. Don't you? Is it frightening? Absolutely, but not nearly as frightening as the truth that staying in a place of comfort will bring about nothing of eternal worth. The worse thing, in my opinion, is missing out on what God is up to in my generation. Eternal impact will be made by us all, positively or negatively, but no one goes through this life without making impact. I want my life to count for Christ.

When God is Silent and Unseen, He still Sees and Hears

Esther's faithfulness in the past gave her the knowledge of how to handle this situation. She would fast, pray and involve others as well. In the midst of her fear, God used her trusted friend, Mordecai, to speak truth to her, to encourage her, to rebuke her and to challenge her. We all need friends like this in our lives, too. God created us for relationship, with Him and with others. And when Mordecai offered his wisdom to her, Esther responded with humility and dependence on God. She didn't depend on her position (she was the queen after all) and she didn't depend on her charm, her personality, or on anything else. She depended on God, and it was His grace that enabled her to say, "If I perish, I perish."

It's very intriguing to me that in this entire story God is never mentioned, nor is prayer even said specifically. It encourages me in my own times of struggle when God seems far away and totally uninvolved in my life. To know that I'm not alone in this kind of experience helps to bring me the courage and hope I need during those seasons to keep pressing in and keep pressing on. I'm learning more and more how important those times are. It seems the greatest spiritual growth often takes place in our lives when we are desperate for a word from God to our hearts and we seem to hit a brick wall rather than the heart of God. Often these kinds of seasons are sent to test our faith and our self-discipline. (Remember what we learned about God's purposes for testing us.) Will we remember all that God has shown us even in those darkest of times? Will we obey even when we feel abandoned by the very One we're running to for rescue? If there is one thing I can say to encourage you, it is this, OBEY!! Please obey, don't give up! It WILL be worth it and I would hate for you to miss out on what God has for you down the road because you "falter(ed) in times of trouble." (Proverbs 24:10 NIV)

God's silences are not an indication that He is playing tricks on you or that He has abandoned you. Those times are absolutely *pregnant* with wonderful things for you to experience and attain. Get out of those seasons everything you can because God is taking you through something very personal and very powerful to strip away at what you may have been holding on to that is keeping you from knowing Him intimately.

We're left to venture a guess as to whether or not God spoke to Esther. As for other people in Scripture who heard from God via angels or even God Himself, we're never told what happened during those three long days of fasting and seeking Yahweh. I can only begin to imagine those 72 hours. Esther was in a place of luxury and power as the queen of Persia, and yet for those three days, I can picture her with tears of anguish in her eyes much of the time as she fervently sought God's will. I imagine that Esther fasted completely, prayed without ceasing, and remembered who she was with a fresh realization that she was a *chosen* woman of God; and that if God had placed her sovereignly in that place, then it would be His sovereignty that would decide her fate. When the moment came to prepare herself to enter the king's court, Esther would have taken her every move very carefully. Just choosing her clothing would be a weighty decision. After having no food for three days, she was probably feeling the physical effects of hunger, grief, and fear. Her courage to obey was not a result of her lack of fear. Her courage was manifest in the fact that she was afraid, and chose to obey anyway.

Divinely Chosen *on* Purpose *for* a Purpose!

Now, with that in mind, let's look at Esther 5:1-2:

"1ON THE third day [of the fast] Esther put on her royal robes and stood in the royal or inner court of the king's palace opposite his [throne room]. The king was sitting on his throne, facing the main entrance of the palace. 2And when the king saw Esther the queen standing in the court, she obtained favor in his sight, and he held out to [her] the golden scepter that was in his hand. So Esther drew near and touched the tip of the scepter." (Amplified Bible)

Some translations say that the king was happy to see Esther, that he was pleased with her, or that she found grace in his eyes. Imagine what was going on inside of her when he not only didn't have her killed immediately, but he was **happy** to see her. Are you breathing a sigh of relief along with her? I do just about every time I read this. I imagine her working up all the courage she can muster before walking in to the king's court, having to remember all she has been taught about etiquette when in the king's presence and having to concentrate on breathing! And then to walk in and be so pleasantly surprised by his response to her...Wow! Can't you picture it? *God wasn't setting her up for failure.* He had divinely placed her right where she was and allowed her to go through all she had because hers was a life on purpose for a purpose. So is yours. Remember the story of three other real-life people we read about in the Old Testament. Their names were Shadrach, Meshach, and Abednego. We read in Daniel 3 that these young men were forced to make a decision, much like Mordecai and the Israelites of his day were forced to make. They could bow to someone or something other than the One True God giving their full allegiance to a false god, or they could die in order to stay true to God. When they were forced to make the decision, the young men replied in this way,

> **"If that *is the case,* our God whom we serve is able to deliver us from the burning fiery furnace, and He will deliver *us* from your hand, O king. 18 But if not, let it be known to you, O king, that we do not serve your gods, nor will we worship the gold image which you have set up."** (Daniel 3:17-18 NKJV)

Like Mordecai and Esther, these young men had a tough decision to make. Something my husband and I have learned and we find ourselves teaching is that one decision equals many choices. When I make one decision, for example, to follow Christ wholeheartedly, I've just made a lifetime of choices. These young men had already made a decision—that they would serve God alone without compromise so when it came time to make a difficult choice, the choice to make was very clear. And then we get to see in Daniel that God not only miraculously spared the lives of these young men, but was found in the fiery furnace with them, and then used their obedience to bring many to faith in God!! Imagine the eternal consequences had they bowed. It is an overwhelming thought. God used their faithfulness to bring others to Himself. Had they chosen to look out for themselves, how many lives would have missed out on eternal salvation?

And, in Esther's story, we read how God protected her as well. And although the name "God" is never mentioned in the book of Esther, we, the readers, clearly see Him throughout the entire story. How often do we need to remember that He is with us even though we can't see Him? Sometimes it takes all of our faith to trust that He is with us when we can't sense His presence with us. I wonder if Esther felt that way as she walked into the king's throne room. It had been so long since he had called for her, and it wasn't the customary thing to do to just show up uninvited; it could have meant her death! Now, can you imagine the sigh of relief that must have come?

Timing is everything---Listen for God's direction!

Let's see what happens next! Read Esther 5:3-8 before moving on.

"3Then the king said to her, What will you have, Queen Esther? What is your request? It shall be given you, even to the half of the kingdom. 4And Esther said, If it seems good to the king, let the king and Haman come this day to the dinner that I have prepared for the king.

5Then the king said, Cause Haman to come quickly, that what Esther has said may be done. 6So the king and Haman came to the dinner that Esther had prepared. 7And during the serving of wine, the king said to Esther, What is your petition? It shall be granted you. And what is your request? Even to the half of the kingdom, it shall be performed. 8Then Esther said, My petition and my request is: If I have found favor in the sight of the king and if it pleases the king to grant my petition and to perform my request, let the king and Haman come tomorrow to the dinner that I shall prepare for them; and I will do tomorrow as the king has said."

Not only was the king thrilled to see his wife, he offered to give her up to half of his kingdom! Now, it would seem that once Esther was in the presence of her husband, the king, and saw his unexpected response, and had Haman right there in their presence, she would have jumped at the opportunity to tell him everything—*but she didn't.* When I have news, good or bad, the main person I want to share it with is my husband. I often answer the phone when he calls during the day and I run through all that I want to tell him and then it dawns on me, "Oops! Maybe I should ask him how he is doing!" So, as you read to this point, what do you think her motive for waiting might have been? Do you think she was overcome with the gravity of the situation and couldn't bring herself to tell-all right then and there? Do you believe she may have been too afraid to let the king know who she was and who her people were? After everything that has happened to get her to this point, she seemingly misses an opportunity to get the word out that Haman wants all of her people annihilated. The king even offered once again to give her anything she wanted, up to half of the kingdom! Common sense would say this was the right time, but God doesn't always go by what makes sense to us. After studying this and praying, I believe the reason she waited was because she was very sensitive to God's perfect timing and to His leading. I believe that somehow, she sensed this just wasn't the right time. And as we read on, we'll find out why.

Something very practical for me to realize as I read this is that there is something to timing things just right.

Confrontations are situations that need to often be handled very delicately. Some consider this to be a form of manipulation, others wisdom. I personally believe the difference between manipulation and wisdom is found in the person's motive for why they are doing what they are doing. For instance, if I have something very important to discuss with my husband that I know will be difficult to handle, I might decide that the best thing to do is to wait until after we've enjoyed a meal as a family and when the house is quieter, perhaps when the kids are all in bed for the night. If my motive is to manipulate the situation to get what I want, then my preparing him a meal and getting the kids to bed will be done with a sinful, manipulative motive. But, if I am doing those very same things in order to make the atmosphere more conducive for both of us to be able to talk unhindered and I submit to the leadership of my husband under God's authority without seeking to fulfill my own agenda, then that is wisdom; same kind of behaviors, different motives. Remember, God sees our hearts.

Prayer: "Dear Father, thank you for your sovereignty. Thank you for the truth that you don't call me to a life of obedience and surrender only to let me down. Thank you for the truth that you are with me in the storms and difficult times. Thank you that you see me even when I don't see you. Grant me wisdom from above to know when to act, when to be silent, and when to speak up. Help me to see when my motives are manipulative rather than wise. Thank you for loving me right where I am, and for loving me too much to leave me here."

Going deeper to understand my Purpose:

1. When Mordecai, Esther, and the three Hebrew boys were faced with their greatest challenge, they stood the test and handled it with courage and integrity because they had been faithful up to that point. What comes to your mind as you consider this? Write down your thoughts in regards to your own personal walk with the Lord in response to this reality.

2. Give a true story from your own life that tells of a time you were challenged to take a stand for Christ and you did. What was the outcome?

3. Has there been a time in your life when you were given a challenge to stand for Christ and you didn't? Recognize that Christ's atonement for sin covers that and you don't have to live under guilt or condemnation, but share what you learned from that experience as well.

Ask Yourself:
4. What is God teaching me?

5. What is my response?

CHAPTER 10

Am I becoming Bitter or Better?
A Lesson of Comparison

Esther 5:9-14

"9Haman went away that day joyful and elated in heart. But when he saw Mordecai at the king's gate refusing to stand up or show fear before him, he was filled with wrath against Mordecai. 10Nevertheless, Haman restrained himself and went home. There he sent and called for his friends and Zeresh his wife. 11And Haman recounted to them the glory of his riches, the abundance of his [ten] sons, all the things in which the king had promoted him, and how he had advanced him above the princes and servants of the king. 12Haman added, Yes, and today Queen Esther did not let any man come with the king to the dinner she had prepared but myself; and tomorrow also I am invited by her together with the king. 13Yet all this benefits me nothing as long as I see Mordecai the Jew sitting at the king's gate. 14Then Zeresh his wife and all his friends said to him, Let a gallows be made, fifty cubits [seventy-five feet] high, and in the morning speak to the king, that Mordecai may be hanged on it; then you go in merrily with the king to the dinner. And the thing pleased Haman, and he caused the gallows to be made." (Amplified Bible)

The "Bitter" Fruit

Haman left feeling very pompous. After all, he had been invited to dine with the king and queen! Of all the royal staff members, men of prominence, governors, etc., only Haman had received a personal invitation to dinner by the queen herself. This fed his ego more than the food fed his appetite! Then he saw Mordecai and had to face the reality that not everyone thought of him as highly as he thought of himself. And, to top it all off, Mordecai showed no fear of him. This absolutely ruined the whole evening for *poor* Haman. When we know we are walking in God's will for our lives, like Mordecai, we don't have to be afraid of opposition either.

In verse 10, we read that Haman "restrained himself." For all those people who think they just can't help themselves from doing the wrong things in their anger, I want to make the point that you can *if you really want to*. Haman was full of hatred, anger, and bitterness, and yet he pulled himself together enough to restrain *himself*. How many times do we give into sinful behaviors because we think we just can't help it? Would we do those very same things if our pastor walked in the door? A child? A respected friend? The truth is that we CAN make choices in behavior. Don't give into the belief that you can't.

We also see that Haman's arrogance kept him from enjoying his prosperity and he became *bitter*. "We are so vain that we even care about the opinion of those we don't care for" (Marie Ebner Von Euschenbach). How true, wouldn't you agree? When Mordecai refused to bow to him, Haman took this as a personal insult. But, he didn't even like Mordecai, so why did it matter? He wasn't secure enough in his position or authority to let it go. As Mordecai went about his life, Haman allowed himself to be eaten up with hatred. This reminds me of the saying "keeping up with the Joneses". How many of us get upset over not being liked by people we don't even like, or know, for that matter? We spend our money, time, resources, emotional energy, physical energy, and more trying to gain acceptance or instill jealousy in people we don't even like! Satan wants to distract us from living the life God has for us and he'll use even our own ridiculousness to do it!

Bitterness robs us of enjoying the pleasures of life

Haman was prosperous, powerful, and popular — but he was PITIFUL. Webster's dictionary defines this in one way as meaning, *"deserving or arousing pity or sympathy."* A friend of mine read this and was concerned about me using the word "pitiful" because she felt it might insult women who I'm also teaching to become more authentic and real, so I want to address this in case you might be thinking the same thing. When we look at the life of Haman, we must remember, he was pitiful because he was living completely in opposition to God. He wasn't humbly confessing to God what his emotions were or going to God and others in relationship to become more like Christ. Haman was his own god and because of this, he was of all people, very pitiful. None of his assets mattered enough to him *to be enough* to keep him satisfied when one man refused to bow in his presence or show fear of him. Why did it have to be such a big deal? It was only one person, but because of Haman's completely self-focused, self-absorbed mind set, one person not bowing to him was like death to his ego, and he couldn't handle it.

Emotions left unchecked can lead to destruction. Haman decides, with the help of his wife, that the only way to feel better about *himself* is to kill *Mordecai* as soon as possible. The people you love the most can be poisoned by the bitterness you refuse to let go. See how Haman's own family was affected by a fight that wasn't even their own?

Bitterness affects my judgment and makes me a poor decision maker

When I am bitter, every decision I make is going to be affected and tainted by my bitterness. I can put on a good show at church even if I'm mad at something someone said, but everything will be affected by it: my ability to worship authentically, my ability to walk in honest relationship with others, even where I'm going to sit or what hall I'll walk down. And, some of us don't even keep our bitterness to ourselves. We sometimes feel that we need to make others aware of the person who hurt us so that we can feel vindicated when our friends rally around us in support. Now, everyone needs a safe person or two who is mature and walking with the Lord to whom they can go for advice and counsel and support, we already talked about this, but be so careful to check your motives. WHY are you going to that person? Are you going to get the word out about what was done to you, or are you going to honestly gain wisdom in how to go about handling this? Are you sincerely going to ask for prayer and counsel or are you going to share gossip and gain support for your "side". Remember what we discussed about our motives in Chapter 9. The very same behaviors can be based on wisdom or manipulation and the difference lies in our motives. God sees our hearts, even when we don't clearly see them for ourselves. He will be faithful to show us what is in our hearts if we'll allow Him that freedom.

My aunt once told me something I've never forgotten. She said, "If you focus on what you don't want to become, you're almost sure to become it because that is what you're focusing on. BUT, if you focus on what you DO want to become, then you're more likely to get there." If you're focusing on the hurts, grudges, offenses, abuses, etc. then you'll never be able to walk away in freedom, but if you'll allow the Lord to be your focus and allow Him to live the Christ-life through you, you'll be amazed at what He will give you the power to do; even the power to let go of anger and bitterness that you've been holding on to for years. It may be an instant deliverance or it may take a long time. Either way, let God be God in your life, and give Him the room to bring freedom to you.

Bitterness destroys the person harboring it, rather than the person receiving it

I've heard this statement many times, but I heard it first from Jay Strack: *"Being bitter is like drinking poison and expecting the other person to die."*

How many of us have dealt with bitterness in our own lives? We know the "spiritual thing" to do is to forgive, so we'll say that we have forgiven someone. We might sincerely believe we have forgiven everyone who has ever wronged us. I want to spend a little bit of time today on this subject of bitterness versus forgiveness. We have discussed bitterness a bit; let's now talk about what forgiveness is, and what forgiveness is not.

I believe the best definition I've ever heard of biblical forgiveness is: *releasing the person who has made the offense from any responsibility to make things even,* or in simpler terms, *releasing them from the debt they owe.* Often times, people think to forgive means to minimize the offense as though it didn't really matter, or it didn't really hurt or offend, when it actually did hurt and it did offend. Biblical forgiveness means that although you were wounded or offended or wronged somehow, you release the person from having to pay you back. You can be honest with how you were impacted by their wounding, and you can be free to express your emotions in a healthy, honorable way. Remember self-control is a fruit of the Spirit and anger is real and normal, but it is not a license to lash out and spew venom on those around you. Sometimes, the flipside of open and obvious bitterness, is that in our quest to be Godly, we offer "forgiveness" without allowing ourselves to process how we may have been impacted by the wrong we were dealt. Depending on the offense, we may need to allow the Lord to search our hearts in order to help us deal with how we were impacted in our beliefs and our behaviors as a result of what was done to us. We may think we've forgiven, but God is faithful and He will show us if we indeed have unforgiveness in our hearts toward another or even several others.

Here is an example that hits close to my home that I hope will make the above statements a little clearer. When my husband was a child, he was sexually abused by an older male for several years of his childhood. It grieves me beyond expression that he endured that kind of abuse. The enemy used that as a powerful weapon against him in many, many ways. When he was 26 years old, and gave his heart and life to Jesus, he knew he needed to forgive that other person for what he had done to him. So, as much as he knew how, he forgave him. Fast forward about 7 years and you'll find Stephen, my husband, having to deal with something else, allowing the Lord to heal him from the effects of the abuse so that he could *fully* forgive the other person. He felt that by saying "I forgive him" that it was done with, but he came to realize that true forgiveness honestly acknowledges the wrong suffered and then goes on to release the other person from being in debt to him. It doesn't mean he has to become best friends with the other person, it doesn't mean he has to pretend it didn't hurt, it doesn't mean he has to reconcile that relationship, but it does mean that he was able, in Christ's sufficiency within him, to release the other person from having to make it up to him. It also freed him from allowing any root of bitterness to spring up within him.

I know of several women who actually pride themselves on how well they can hold grudges as though this were some kind of Olympic sport and they were after the Gold Medal!! They'll say, "I'll tell you one thing, if you cross me, then that's it!" These are women who never learned that forgiveness doesn't empower the other person to abuse you again. It doesn't mean that the hurt didn't matter. It doesn't mean they "got away with it", whatever "it" was. Bitterness is the shackles you place on *your own feet*, chaining you forever to the event and the person who wounded you and profoundly affects your ability to walk freely in your calling to live the abundant life of Christ. Forgiveness is the key that unlocks you from the shackles and sets you free to move on and grow.

I've told my children, as they have had to learn to forgive AND to *accept* forgiveness, that forgiveness means we don't keep bringing it up and that the matter is settled. They don't need to expect something from the one who hurt them, nor do they need to expect us, their parents, to want payment for how they may have offended us.

We can forgive even without an apology from the one who hurt us. Sometimes the wounds that go the deepest are the ones caused by someone who will never say "I realize how much I've hurt you, and I'm deeply sorry." Wouldn't it be a great thing if people would always own up to the hurts they've inflicted on us? Knowing what someone should do and desiring that they do it is not sinful, but holding onto the desire and creating a demand out of it can be a sin which will continue to rob you and those around you from the spiritual blessings God has for you. God is faithful, and He is powerful. If you are struggling in this area, let Him bring freedom to your soul by acknowledging the truth that there is bitterness in your heart. Give Him the privilege of helping you release the offender of his/her debt to you so that YOU might walk in joy and freedom.

When we are the one who has brought about the offense, then scripture does teach us that we need to make amends however we can. Scripture clearly teaches that each person is responsible for his/her own personal choices and behaviors. I have found that it is often more difficult for me to forgive myself than it is to forgive others. I usually feel as though if I forgive myself, I'm letting myself off of a hook on which I deserve to remain indefinitely—at least until I pay for my crime! I heard someone say once that if we will allow ourselves to receive God's grace in His forgiveness— if we will accept His forgiveness that He shed His blood to provide—it is more powerful than striving to forgive ourselves. As I am reminded of the stupid and sinful things I have done, it becomes a choice of the will to accept that Jesus' blood shed for me was completely sufficient. I need not—I dare not—insult my Lord and my God by imagining that I might have something of worth to offer through keeping myself in turmoil or bondage over my sins that would add value on top of what He did so completely. I heard of a survey several years ago that asked Americans what they're favorite words were to hear. The first one by and large was "I love you" and the second is no surprise to me either, "I forgive you". Forgiveness is an amazing and beautiful gift—whether given or received.

I want to make one point here while it's on my mind. **Forgiveness is often times a *process* rather than an event.** If someone cuts me off in traffic, I can pretty easily forgive them and move on with my life. But there are some hurts, some offenses, that are so painful to even look at fully, that sometimes the process takes days, weeks, months, even years. Being in the process and asking the Lord to help you forgive is definitely going to move you away from allowing bitterness to grow in you. You can't grow in forgiveness and bitterness at the same time, but don't be discouraged in reading this that you have to have a completely clean slate with every offense today. I do hope you are encouraged to allow the Lord to work in your life and take you through the process of forgiving. Bitterness keeps you harnessed to the person who hurt you and you'll never be free until you take the steps of forgiving. Just like everything else, what God calls us to do, God empowers and enables us to do. He won't leave you to your own abilities; He will faithfully guide you and keep you and lead you through the often-times painful struggles of offering forgiveness. (Don't be opposed to seeking help through a biblical counseling center if you need someone to walk with you through the process of forgiving.)

Scripture warns us of the dangers of allowing a root of bitterness to develop in our lives. (Heb. 12: 14-15) Although one might feel a sense of empowerment when harboring bitterness, the reality is that he/she has allowed himself/herself to become enslaved. Everything is driven by that bitterness, not by freedom. Bitterness is completely self-focused. Even when the plot is revealed, (as we'll see in the next chapter), Haman is still making poor choices by not honoring Queen Esther. His self-focused lifestyle was his undoing. He allowed himself to become enslaved to bitterness. Every decision he made was born out of his bitterness. And as we'll see as the story unfolds, it ruined HIS life, not the life of the one to whom he was bitter.

The "Better" Fruit

Becoming better means I can enjoy my life and be content in whatever circumstances I find myself living in (apart from rebellion). Philippians 4:11-13.

Mordecai's and Esther's acceptance of their roles in God's Kingdom enabled them to become *better*. Rather than focusing on what they didn't have or couldn't do, they lived out of their identity as God's children. Choosing God's way causes me to grow and to become better. God wants me to obey Him because I've learned to trust Him. There is a song we used to sing in church when I was a kid that is probably at least somewhat familiar to you. It goes like this, "Learning to lean, I'm learning to lean, learning to lean on Jesus. Finding more power than I ever dreamed, I'm learning to lean on Jesus." Learning to lean on Jesus takes time in relationship. One thing I learned during my divorce was that sometimes I have to CHOOSE with my mind to believe God's Word. Sometimes, it doesn't FEEL like I can trust Him. Sometimes it FEELS like God isn't there or that if He is, He doesn't care. I have never regretted making the choice to obey His Word even when my feelings were telling me to run from Him, to run from this God who would allow me to be hurt in such a devastating way. But, through it all there was the resolve to trust Him anyway, and I am so thankful that I did. I have never obeyed perfectly, but consistent faithfulness has helped me to grow better instead of bitter. And, because of the tough decision to obey God, even when it hurt, I have reaped the rewards of wonderful relationships, greater intimacy with God and a much deeper level of trust in Him. As I choose to obey and follow His ways, my faith is strengthened for the journey. God wants to take each of us deeper, but if we allow bitterness to develop, we stunt our own growth. Mordecai and Esther never became bitter. They didn't try to retaliate against Haman and his family, but they did decide they were going to trust God to protect them and the other Israelites. They left vengeance to God which is where it belongs. God can take care of avenging us far better than we can anyway.

Mordecai and Esther were also willing to patiently wait on the Lord's timing. In choosing to accept delayed gratification rather than running ahead and trying to take care of things in their own wisdom and their own strength, they trusted that God would make a way. "Better" leads to eternal and lasting rewards. It isn't focused so heavily on the here and now, but is eternity minded, realizing that the God who sees the end from the beginning and loves us, has a purpose for everything He allows. Others, too, benefit from my obedience and trust in the Lord. ALL of the Jews were spared. And, in addition, you and I have been affected! *"The lineage of Jesus Christ was preserved through Esther's obedience!"*

Becoming better is worth what it takes to get me there

Sometimes God seems unkind and unjust. We see some thrive while we struggle, or we thrive while others barely get by and we wonder why God doesn't do things that are more "fair". God is not fair; He never claimed to be fair. He is just. He is very personal and knows exactly what circumstances and situations to take us through to make us more like Jesus, more like the people we are created to be. We cannot be content, joyful, or satisfied outside of God's will, regardless of what our circumstances might be. Haman had everything and was still not satisfied. Becoming better always has others in mind. No man is an island. We all cast a shadow.

Becoming "better", a more mature Christian, a more devoted follower of Jesus Christ, **is worth the painful events that God uses to get me there**. I wouldn't wish my life's pain on anyone else, I'm sure you feel the same way about what you've experienced that has wounded you. But, I wouldn't trade what I know now . I wouldn't trade this intimacy or understanding gained, for *anything*. No "Easy Street" lifestyle yields the rewards that I've been given *THROUGH* the pain. If you were to talk to my husband about the abuse he endured as a child, he would tell you it was horrible, but he would also tell you how God has healed him from the pain, the shame, the anger, and the embarrassment of it all. This is God's mercy. God didn't stop there, but He has also made his ministry to men with life-dominating bondage more effective as a result of his ability to identify with their pain, their shame, and their anger—THAT is God's grace!

When God called me to teach and write, He said at one point in the process, "Shelley, if you take all of your assets and add them all up and then try to minister out of your own strength, those assets will become your greatest liabilities. BUT, if you'll surrender all of your liabilities to me (the fact that you experienced sexual abuse, the fact that you're divorced, the fact that you never went to college, the fact that you still miss the mark) if you'll give it all to me and allow my Holy Spirit to work through you, then those things you see as your liabilities will become your greatest assets." I recently heard Beth Moore say at a Ministry Wives Conference in 2006, "We are better people *healed* than we ever would have been *well*." I couldn't agree more.

My friends, which path are you on today? Are you on The Path of Bitterness or the Path of Becoming Better?

Prayer: "Father, thank you for your Word that cuts, but also heals. Show me where I have any bitterness, and please give me strength and courage to release it to you. Where you have brought healing thus far, I thank you"

Going Deeper to Understand My Purpose

1. List what you see as your greatest assets:

2. List what you would define as your greatest liabilities:

3. Now, read II Corinthians 4:7; here it is for you in the Amplified Bible Translation: *"7However, we possess this precious treasure [the divine Light of the Gospel] in [frail, human] vessels of earth, that the grandeur and exceeding greatness of the power may be shown to be from God and not from ourselves."*

4. When you take an honest look at your strengths and liabilities, God wants you to be willing to surrender it all to Him. After all, you are a vessel which houses the very glory of God! Let His nature, His divine Light, shine through you—the cracks and blemishes of that earthen vessel, surrendered to a holy God, makes for a better lamp to shine forth His glory!! Write down your response to this reality:

5. Is there any bitterness in your own heart toward someone?

6. Are you willing to allow God to remove that through your confession to Him and repentance from it? Explain your answer.

7. Is there someone whose forgiveness you long to have, but you've never been given? Tell it to Jesus, and then share this with your small group. You may never receive the person's forgiveness, but wholeness and healing are still available through Christ.

CHAPTER 11

The Truth Comes Out—Finally!!

⌒

Esther 6 & 7

*T*his is where I get so excited! (Have I said that before? I love this story!) It is so wonderful to me that God doesn't only give us part of the story—He lets us see how it all works out. When I go through the difficult times in my life, I can look at Scripture and the lives of other believers who may be further in their journey with the Lord and I can be encouraged to see how God works out His good plans. (See James 5:10-11) Sometimes God refreshes my faith by allowing me to see the change He makes in the life of a lost person when that person accepts Christ into his/her own life. It is so exciting and encouraging to see believers grow!

When we left Esther at the first banquet, we considered the reason or reasons that kept her from telling everything to her husband, the king, at that time. Well, we may not know exactly what was going through her mind that kept it from happening, but we're going to get some insight into God's reasons. His timing can be trusted because HE can be trusted. Let's get into Chapter 6—I can hardly wait!!

"1That night the king couldn't sleep. He ordered the record book, the day-by-day journal of events, to be brought and read to him. 2They came across the story there about the time that Mordecai had exposed the plot of Bigthana and Teresh--the two royal eunuchs who guarded the entrance and who had conspired to assassinate King (Ahasuerus). 3The king asked, "What great honor was given to Mordecai for this?" "Nothing," replied the king's servants who were in attendance. "Nothing has been done for him." 4The king said, "Is there anybody out in the court?" Now Haman had just come into the outer court of the king's palace to talk to the king about hanging Mordecai on the gallows he had built for him. 5The king's servants said, "Haman is out there, waiting in the court." "Bring him in," said the king. 6When Haman entered, the king said, "What would be appropriate for the man the king especially wants to honor?" Haman thought to himself, "He must be talking about honoring me-- who else?" 7So he answered the king, "For the man the king delights to honor, do this: 8Bring a royal robe that the king has worn and a horse the king has ridden, one with a royal crown on its head. 9Then give the robe and the horse to one of the king's most noble princes. Have him robe the man whom the king especially wants to honor; have the prince lead him on horseback through the city square, proclaiming before him, "This is what is done for the man whom the king especially wants to honor!'" 10"Go and do it," the king said to Haman. "Don't waste another minute. Take the robe and horse and do what you have proposed to Mordecai the Jew who sits at the King's Gate. Don't leave out a single detail of your plan." 11So Haman took the robe and horse; he robed Mordecai and led him through the city square, proclaiming before him, "This is what is done for the man whom the king especially wants to honor!" 12Then Mordecai returned to the King's Gate, but Haman fled to his house, thoroughly morti- fied, hiding his face. 13When Haman had finished telling his wife Zeresh and all his friends everything that had happened to him, his knowledgeable friends who were there and his wife Zeresh said, "If this Mordecai is in fact a Jew, your bad luck has only begun. You don't stand a chance against him--you're as good as ruined." 14While they were still talking, the king's eunuchs arrived and hurried Haman off to the dinner that Esther had prepared." (The Message Translation; used because of its beautiful wording in this passage.)

God's Timing can be Trusted because GOD can be trusted!

Oh, wow! I wish so much I could have been there!! God's timing was so perfect. Look at all the seemingly coincidental things that took place in this one chapter. First, the king has insomnia, (even peaceful sleep is a gift from God), so he asks his servant to read what he considers to be boring and monotonous enough to get him to sleep, and just what does this servant *happen* to read? He recites the chronicles which tell of all the happenings in the kingdom, and what portion of this does he just *happen* to read that very night-- the account of how Mordecai had saved the life of the king by thwarting the plans of the two thugs who wanted to kill Ahasuerus! Friends, God is sovereign!! You can trust Him to do what is right and what is just. You may have to wait what seems like forever, but He will come through and it will be at the perfect time and in the perfect way.

When my oldest child was a toddler, there was a time that we had a bit of a drive to make. I knew it would be a long one for her, so I stopped at a drive-thru and got us a soft drink to share on the way. Because she was still so young, and seated behind me in her car seat, I kept the drink up front with me in a cup holder with plans to give her a turn getting a sip when we made our stops at traffic lights and stop signs—which I knew would be a lot! From her inexperienced, young, and even immature perspective (which was natural, she was 2!), she thought I was holding out on her and pitched the biggest fit for her turn of having a sip of the beverage. I remember so clearly seeing a light turning red, only seconds away, and trying to explain to her that she would get her turn very soon, that I had bought this drink with her in mind, and that I *wanted* to give it to her. She was fussing so much; she couldn't even hear me trying to talk to her to calm her down with the truth. From my perspective, she only had seconds to wait for something that I was more than happy to give to her. I knew that if I gave it to her at the moment when she was demanding it, it would spill all over her and the car and she wouldn't really enjoy it as much if that happened. (Nor would I for that matter!) In that moment, I remember so clearly hearing God whisper to my heart, "Shelley, you do the same thing. You often believe I'm holding out on you, or that I've said 'no' about something, when often times the truth is that I have that very desire waiting for the right time to give it to you. You make such a fuss that you don't realize I'm trying to speak to you. And you think you're going to have to wait forever, when from My perspective, it is closer than you can imagine. If I give it to you too soon, you might just make a mess of it!" I don't think I'll ever forget that lesson God gave me that day. Friend, our God is a trustworthy God—trust Him, and trust His timing.

God's Sovereignty Can be Trusted...

Next, we see another "coincidence". As the king finds out that nothing has been done to honor Mordecai for this act of bravery and loyalty to the king, and as he is just beginning to think of what could be done for him, Haman is coming to see the king (in the middle of the night!) to find out if he can KILL Mordecai. I wish I could have been a fly on that wall! So, then, when Haman comes in, the king says to him in not so many words, "Hey friend, if you were going to honor someone very special to the king, in a very special way, how would you go about doing that?" And, Haman, being the totally self-focused man that he was, couldn't *imagine* there could be anyone the king would want to honor more than *him*, so he gives in great detail what he thinks the king should do, all the while, getting prouder and prouder, imagining all of this being done for him. He went into such explicit detail of the fantasy he had knowing he would enjoy being the center of not only his own world, but, at least for a short time, being the center of everyone else's as well. Can you picture this? Then, shock of all shocks: the king says, "Great idea—perfect—do all of this exactly as you've described for *Mordecai!*" I wonder how Haman kept his composure in front of the king. I wonder how far his chin dropped when he stepped around the corner out of view of others. What must have been going through his mind? He didn't have time to do much else but put the plans into action to honor his enemy. He was the very one the king chose to parade Mordecai through the kingdom. I love a good story— especially when it is true! I can imagine that the only thing that helped him keep his cool through this whole thing was the other fantasy he was playing over and over in his mind— the one where he would publicly humiliate Mordecai and all of his people on the 13th day of Adar. For Haman, it couldn't arrive quickly enough!

As soon as the parade for Mordecai was over, Haman went home thoroughly disgusted, humiliated, and mortified. Another ironic thing to me is how quickly his wife changed her tune. Just the night before she advised him to build the gallows and just have Mordecai killed, as though it was some simple solution that would solve all of Haman's woes. Now she is speaking with more sense. I wonder what must have been going on the night before. Did she just want to get

Haman to be quiet so she could sleep? Was she sick of hearing this and just said what sounded good at the time? Whatever the case, she now realized that Haman had set himself up against a child of God. She had seen enough to know that messing with a child of God would only end up in trouble for the one who was doing the "messing". She warned her husband, but he still didn't listen. Immediately, he was taken to his banquet with the king and queen, probably appeasing his hatred and soothing his wounded ego with the thoughts of this great honor of dining with the king and queen that was *just for him*.

There are so many lessons for us in this whole story and in this chapter. Here are just a few:

❖ First, God sees all. He knows what you're going through, and what you've been through. He knows what you have done and what has been done to you. Submit to Him so that you, too, can get in on what He is doing. If we choose to remain bitter over the past, we cannot fully enjoy the blessings of today.

❖ God is still in charge. No one gets to be sovereign except for God Almighty. He not only sees, but He is in control. He doesn't sit idly by and just watch humanity run the world. He is in control and will make all things work together for good to those who love Him. (See Romans 8:28.)

❖ God will use even the wickedness of others to bring about His good will. Does this mean He authors their sin? I don't believe that at all. What I do believe is that since God sees each person at the core of who they are, and sees their heart, whether it is for Him or not, He will use a wicked person's choices, or a person's wicked choices whichever you prefer, to bring about His will.

Now, let's get back to the story and read how the second banquet goes.

Esther 7

"1 So the king and Haman went to Queen Esther's banquet. 2 On this second occasion, while they were drinking wine, the king again said to Esther, "Tell me what you want, Queen Esther. What is your request? I will give it to you, even if it is half the kingdom!" 3 Queen Esther replied, "If I have found favor with the king, and if it pleases the king to grant my request, I ask that my life and the lives of my people will be spared. 4 For my people and I have been sold to those who would kill, slaughter, and annihilate us. If we had merely been sold as slaves, I could remain quiet, for that would be too trivial a matter to warrant disturbing the king." 5 "Who would do such a thing?" King (Ahasuerus) demanded. "Who would be so presumptuous as to touch you?" 6 Esther replied, "This wicked Haman is our adversary and our enemy." Haman grew pale with fright before the king and queen. 7 Then the king jumped to his feet in a rage and went out into the palace garden. Haman, however, stayed behind to plead for his life with Queen Esther, for he knew that the king intended to kill him. 8 In despair he fell on the couch where Queen Esther was reclining, just as the king was returning from the palace garden. The king exclaimed, "Will he even assault the queen right here in the palace, before my very eyes?" And as soon as the king spoke, his attendants covered Haman's face, signaling his doom. 9 Then Harbona, one of the king's eunuchs, said, "Haman has set up a sharpened pole that stands seventy-five feet tall in his own courtyard. He intended to use it to impale Mordecai, the man who saved the king from assassination." "Then impale Haman on it!" the king ordered. 10 So they impaled Haman on the pole he had set up for Mordecai, and the king's anger subsided." (The Message)

God's Justice Can Be Trusted

Wow! What an ironic turn of events, wouldn't you agree? Impaling a person on a gallows was not only fatal and painful physically, it also served as a way to publicly humiliate a person in his death. Not only that, but it was meant to shame and dishearten the family members of the one(s) killed. Haman didn't just want to kill Mordecai, although that was a pretty significant thing in and of itself, he wanted to destroy Mordecai and any and everything that Mordecai stood for. Proverbs 21:30 says, *"There is no wisdom, no insight, no plan that can succeed against the LORD."* When Haman set himself against Mordecai, he was actually making himself an enemy of Almighty God. God will not sit idly by and do nothing when His faithful people are being victimized. God is a God of justice and He will repay. We *can* trust Him to do what is best in every situation we face.

God's Purposes Can Be Trusted...

God granted Esther, and even Mordecai, favor with King Ahasuerus. He didn't give them this gift merely for their own enjoyment. He blessed them in order to use them to rescue an entire people group. In our Western culture, we often see blessings as an end in and of themselves. We work, struggle, and fantasize about all the things we want and don't have or have and don't want. We compare our lives with those around us who either have more than we do or less and we become competitors rather than companions in our constant comparing. (Try to say that three times really fast!) We need to remember that God's purposes are much bigger than that. God is about His Kingdom, not our little kingdoms. Had Esther or Mordecai been as self-focused in this season of their lives as Haman was, the story would have been a very different story. God would still have rescued His people (Esther 4), but the name of the book would not have been "Esther". I for one do not want to miss out on the purpose God has for me. I want to remember that I am part of something much bigger than just myself, or just my family, or just my neighborhood, or my church, etc. I am part of God's Eternal Kingdom. What I have, I have because He has given it to me, partly to bless me, but mostly to bless me *even more* by using me to bless those around me. If we know Jesus personally as our personal Lord and Savior, then we're part of the "Body" of Christ. We're not independent of one another; we're a *part* of one another. So, when one suffers, all suffer, and when one rejoices, we should all rejoice.

God has spoken to my heart recently in this very area. Some friends of ours have chosen to bless us with financial gifts as they seek to encourage and bless us as we seek to encourage and bless through ministering to the Body of Christ. Several people have done for us, financially, what we are not in a position to do for ourselves. God has chosen to give to us through their hands, and it has truly blessed and ministered to us. When I was thinking recently about how much I want to be in a position to give financially like that and to bless others in the same ways I have been blessed, God reminded me by speaking to my spirit: "Shelley, always remember it all comes from Me. Whether you write the check or someone else writes it, I am the Provider of it all. You have everything you need today to do everything I've called you to do *today*." That has freed me up so much. To be surrendered *today*, to be faithful *today*, and maybe, just maybe,

God will bring me to a place where I can do more for Him and for others. But for *today,* He has called me to be faithful with what I already do have from Him. What do you have from the Lord that He has blessed you with to enjoy, but also to share? It may be financial prosperity, it may be a special talent, it may be a home with empty rooms to share....whatever it is, be faithful *today* with those gifts. God sees and God cares and God remembers it all. You may never know in this lifetime the lives you've touched, but God sees and knows every single one and He is keeping a record of it all.

GOD can be trusted!!

> *Prayer: "Heavenly Father, thank you for the truth and the reminder that You really can be trusted in all things. Thank you for the reality that You are good and You do good—that You can't NOT do what is best in every situation. Help me to trust You more as I seek to know You more. Let me never settle for less than Your absolute best."*

Going Deeper to Understand My Purpose

1. What is the area in your life where you sense the greatest need for God's provision, protection, or touch?

2. Describe an event or situation that you have personally experienced, first-hand, that God used to deepen and strengthen your personal faith and trust in Him.

A. How did you feel during the event?

B. What did you learn through the event?

C. How is your relationship with God different on this side of the event?

3. 2 Corinthians 1:3-4 says, "3 Praise be to the God and Father of our Lord Jesus Christ, the Father of compassion and the God of all comfort, 4 who comforts us in all our troubles, so that we can comfort those in any trouble with the comfort we ourselves have received from God." (NIV)

   A. With this verse in mind, describe an event in your life in which you felt the compassion and comfort of God Himself.

B. How has He used you to bring comfort to others as a result of this comfort He brought you?

C. Again, with this passage in mind, describe and event in your life where you were comforted by someone else who showed compassion to you.

4. What is the main thing God saying to you today?

5. What will you do in response to what God is saying to you?

CHAPTER 12

The Rest of the Story...
Esther Chapters 7-9

How Ironic!

*I*n Chapter 7 of the book of Esther, we read that the truth *finally* came out. Esther was able to tell her husband what was about to happen to her people, and then was able to disclose Haman's true motives and wickedness. More irony: the very gallows he had built to hang Mordecai upon would be where he would breathe his last breath. All that energy, intelligence, leadership potential was completely wasted. Haman's undoing was his own pride. As I said in the very beginning of this book, this story is better than any fairy tale because this story is completely true!

In Chapter 8, we see where Mordecai was given everything Haman had owned or managed just moments before. God sees it all, my friend. He sees when we are serving Him with right motives, when we make sacrifices to honor Him, when we suffer in order to do what is right. He sees and He remembers. Humility always precedes true honor. (See Proverbs 15:33 and Proverbs 18:12) God exalts in *due time*, and always when we have come in humility. (I Peter 5:6) Mordecai had faithfully served God as a parent and protector to Esther. He had served God faithfully as a man unwilling to bend the knee to anyone other than to God, even when he knew it could cost him everything. He humbly accepted recognition from the king and didn't gloat when his enemy had to lead him around proclaiming his favor with the king. (It would have been so hard for me to not do that!) Mordecai wasn't a perfect man, but he was a faithful man. This is good news for each of us! We, too, can choose to be humble, to be faithful, and to be yielded to God. *This isn't something only for a select few, but sadly, only a few tend to choose to live this way.* I hope and pray you will be one of those few. Remember this: Mordecai was the only one listed as unwilling to bow to Haman and a whole nation was saved as a result! Not only was the nation spared, but we see in the rest of the chapter, that the nation was exalted above where it had been for so long. Our obedience and surrender to God can impact an entire nation. I want so much to see my home country positively impacted as a result of my willingness to be a surrendered vessel for God's purposes. Can you imagine if more of us would decide to live lives on purpose for a purpose? It's incredible to think of what God could do in our nation, for the generations to come, with an individual or group with that level of commitment to Him.

A New Law

Because of the king's trust in Esther and in Mordecai, the Jews were given the freedom to fight back, to defend themselves. They were given the authority they needed to win the battle that was appointed for them by Haman. Because the decree had been signed into law by the king, not even the king could undo it. But, *he could write a new one*!

Read this in Esther 8:11-17

"11In it the king granted the Jews who were in every city to gather and defend their lives; to destroy, to slay, and to wipe out any armed force that might attack them, their little ones, and women; and to take the enemies' goods for spoil. 12On one day in all the provinces of King Ahasuerus, the thirteenth day of the twelfth month, the month of Adar, 13A copy of the writing was to be issued as a decree in every province and as a proclamation to all peoples, and the Jews should be ready on that day to avenge themselves upon their enemies. 14So the couriers, who were mounted on swift beasts that were used in the king's service, went out, being hurried and urged on by the king's command; and the decree was released in Shushan, the capital. 15And Mordecai went forth from the presence of the king in royal apparel of blue and white, with a great crown of gold and with a robe of fine linen and purple; and the city of Shushan shouted and rejoiced. 16The Jews had light [a dawn of new hope] and gladness and joy and honor. 17And in every province and in every city, wherever the king's command and his decree came, the Jews had gladness and joy, a feast and a holiday. And many from among the peoples of the land [submitted themselves to Jewish rite and] became Jews, for the fear of the Jews had fallen upon them." (Amplified Bible)

There is so much in this passage! I love this!! We have already discussed how Satan's plans parallel Haman's plans, but here, we get to see a parallel with God's plan of redemption! Because of sin, we are all born under one kind of law. A law that says we have to meet every point of the righteous requirements of God or we will live forever, eternally separated from God. God cannot undo that law—He wrote it! But, because He is God, He has authority to write one that gives us a way of escape from that original law. When Jesus lived a perfect, sinless life, was punished on our behalf in his death on the cross, and then was resurrected by God to life, we were given access to a new decree, a new law! Now, when we read that first decree, like the Jews of Esther's day, we feel helpless. There is nothing we can do; this is the law! But, also like the Jews, when we read the second decree, we can rejoice and celebrate because now there is hope!! Now there is a provision for our salvation by way of the new law—the New Covenant.

Secondly, we see that when the Jews acted under the provisions of the second decree, many people became Jews. When unbelievers saw the power and provision of God in the way He protected His people, it drew unbelievers to God. God works in this same way today. When God's people live under the new law of liberty and behave out of their true identity as a child of God, non-believers will notice and many will be drawn to God, too. Do people who know you see God at work? Do they see you living out of the reality of who God says you are? Are they drawn to this very good, very powerful One you claim has rescued you from the first law?

The last illustration I want to discuss is that this second law allowed the people to be ready when the attack would come. Just because you become a believer doesn't mean that all the attacks on your life will stop or that opposition will cease to come. In fact, more than likely, the attacks will increase and the opposition will intensify. BUT, you and I do not have to be afraid. We get to prepare in advance. When we expect it, it makes it much less frightening, especially when we remember God's sovereignty. He uses the painful things, the difficult things, *all things*, to bring about His good and perfect will. So, don't give in to fear. Speak truth to your fear when you feel it rising up in you. The Jewish people affected by these two decrees were allowed to take up weapons, prepare for battle and then fight with God Almighty on their side, and they WON! They still had to fight, but victory was theirs for the claiming! Do you see the parallel? THAT is exciting to me!

Devastation turned to Celebration!

Lastly, in Chapter 9 we see that God indeed gave victory to His people, and it happened on the very day Haman had planned for their complete annihilation. Another word that could have been used for this book is "Irony"; this whole story is full of irony! Even to the point that the celebration that Jews still celebrate to remember this victory is called "The Feast of Purim" which means the "Feast of the Lots" because the lots were cast by Haman to decide on the date of battle and the Jews were spared and set free on that very day. Haman, the enemy, meant this to be a day for evil against the people of God. But God saw past what Haman or anyone else could see. He saw "the end intended of the Lord" (James 5:10-11) and saw what this day would really mean for His people and the generations that followed.

Queen Esther and Mordecai served their God and their king very well. Although we never read that Ahasuerus ever became a believer, we see how God provided for Mordecai and Esther and gave them a full life on the earth. If you are married to an unbelieving spouse, continue to love that one with the love of Christ and walk in the wisdom available to you. Trust God with your spouse.

Final thoughts...

As we close this study, I want to point out something out that meant a lot to me. In verse 4, we read that "Mordecai had become increasingly prominent." Does this mean that he no longer had any enemies and that everyone thought he was wonderful? More than likely the answer is no. But because he was a man of great integrity and faithfulness, even those who didn't like him still had reason to respect him. As a *board certified people pleaser* I am impacted by this in a profound way. Someone wise once taught me that sometimes the best thing you can do for yourself and others is to give people permission to dislike you. As you seek to be a person of faithfulness, to God, to your Christian brothers and sisters, to your family members, to God's call upon your life, keep in mind that not everyone is going to agree with everything you do or always even *like* you. They won't always believe in what you're doing and support your service for God. They won't necessarily appreciate you or what God is doing in and through you. You may be wounded by those who mistreat you because of your stand for Christ, even by those who claim Him as their personal Lord and Savior as well. And, unfortunately, the more you walk in freedom, the more those who are still in bondage will try to bring you back to the stocks with them. People tend to be creatures of habit and tend to have a difficult time accepting change, even if it is good change; it often feels more *spiritual* to be unhappy.

Mother Teresa said, *"People are often unreasonable, illogical, and self-centered; forgive them anyway. If you are kind, people may accuse you of selfish, ulterior motives; be kind anyway. If you are successful, you will win some false friends and true enemies; succeed anyway. If you are honest and frank, people may cheat you; be honest and frank*

anyways. What you spent years building, someone could destroy overnight; build anyway. If you find serenity and happiness, they may be jealous; be happy anyway. The good you do today, people will often forget tomorrow; do good anyway. Give the world the best you have and it may never be enough; give the world the best you have anyway. You see, in the final analysis, it is between you and God; it was never between you and them anyway."(Internet Source, http://www.zaadz.com, quoted from Mother Teresa of Calcutta)

Take heart, my friend, as you continue to live in humility before God and man, that you, too, can become increasingly prominent and make an eternal impact to mark your place in this generation. And, as God used Esther and Mordecai to set His people free and to bring many to faith in God, your story in Heaven can read much the same way!

As we come to the end of this study about the lives of Esther, Mordecai, King Ahasuerus, Haman, and Vashti, along with the others we've discussed, I wonder where you might be on this side of the study in relation to where you were spiritually, mentally, and emotionally before you began this journey with me. My deep desire and prayer is that you've come to recognize in a fresh and exciting way that God really, really does love you; that He really is for you; that His purposes and plans, although painful and frightening to us at times, are always and forever for our good and His glory, that He might bring others to Himself and each of us *home*. When we chose the cover of this book, wanting a picture that would in some way depict artistically the message of the book, we chose the drop of water that splashed into the shape of a crown. To me, this portrays Esther's life so simply and yet so beautifully. All of the things she experienced in life up to the point of recognizing her destiny were chosen to bring about God's intended purposes. All of the different life experiences and circumstances may have seemed less significant while she was going through them than they really were. But, as we've seen in this study, everything led her to a place of royalty that she might make full use of her position as queen. My friend, if you know Christ as your savior, then you can rest assured that God is using it all—even the things that seem to be meaningless and pointless—to bring about His good purposes for you. And, as a child of God, you, too, are royalty! *Please do not waste that position.* You are needed!

I pray that this time in study and reflecting on the truths of God's word has brought you into greater intimacy with this amazing God who deeply desires to walk in intimacy with you. And that when, *not if*, the trials and temptations and tests of this life come your way, you'll be able to stand firm for this One who has stood firm for you and that you will remember: you are here *On Purpose, For a Purpose*!!

Now, I invite you to go live like it!

Prayer: "Dear Heavenly Father—Thank you for your word that is alive and powerful—your word that changes us from the inside-out. I pray that You will continue this good work you've begun in me and that you will strengthen me in the inner person to live my life on purpose—for the purpose of knowing you more and glorifying you in my life. Use me to be a voice in my generation!"

Going Deeper to Understand my Purpose

Please take a few minutes to write out your personal response to this study while it's still fresh on your mind.

1. What have you learned that you'll never forget? What is the main truth that will stick with you long after this study is over?

2. How have you been impacted by this study's overall theme that God is a God of purpose?

3. How will the truths of this study affect you as you seek to be a personal witness for the Gospel of Jesus Christ?

4. What changes, if any, have taken place in your personal spiritual warfare tactics?

5. Lasting impressions...

$\mathcal{W}$e would love to hear from you! It would bless us at "Mary's Vineyard Ministries, Inc." to hear how God has used this Bible Study in your life. If you'd like to take a moment to write to us, please visit our website at www.shelleyhendrix.com

For information on purchasing the "On Purpose For A Purpose" video series that accompanies this book, please contact us through our website or call us at 770-877-0007.

Shelley Hendrix has spoken at various events, conferences, banquets, and retreats throughout the U.S. For information on booking Shelley Hendrix to speak at your event, please log onto www.shelleyhendrix.com. We look forward to hearing from you soon!

Shelley Hendrix is also the co-creator and speaker for the "Get Real Conferences" for women together with her partner, Erica Branch, (www.ericabranch.com) who leads the conference worship time. God is greatly using this conference series throughout the US. The "Get Real Conference" is a flexible conference package that comes to minister alongside of the local church in reaching women with the Good News of Jesus Christ, utilizing Powerful and Authentic Worship, along with Passionate and Timely Messages from God's Word that engage, encourage and challenge the conference attendees. Get more information on the conference, along with booking information, by logging onto www.shelleyhendrix.com

Printed in the United States
87888LV00002B/169-999/A